How to Fix Nigeria

AND MAKE IT WORK FOR EVERY NIGERIAN

UCHE NWAKUDU

authorHOUSE®

AuthorHouse™
1663 Liberty Drive
Bloomington, IN 47403
www.authorhouse.com
Phone: 1-800-839-8640

First published by AuthorHouse   6/15/2011

ISBN: 978-1-4634-0690-5 (e)
ISBN: 978-1-4634-0691-2 (sc)

Library of Congress Control Number: 2011908558

Printed in the United States of America

Dedicated to the memory of my beloved father
Samuel Ndubueze Nwakudu
1923 - 2010

Who taught me that wisdom comes from observation and forethought and that forthrightness is the cornerstone of a progressive community

HOW TO FIX NIGERIA

Fixing Nigeria is a daunting proposition that will take spirited effort, require heavy lifting, and take some time to accomplish, but it is doable.

Fixing Nigeria is possible because every single Nigerian knows that Nigeria is in a sorry state of systemic, structural, socio-political and economic disrepair and every single Nigerian agrees that Nigeria needs fixing. The only thing that has been lacking is a clear and sensible way of going about it.

If there is any chance that Nigeria can be purged of the many malaises that plague her, it lies within the pages of this book.

The book is Nigeria unraveled! It succinctly articulates the cogent problems with the country and proffers well reasoned, salient, and practical ways about how the country can be reformed and made to work for all of its citizens rather than a few privileged people.

Here, for every Nigerian who has dreamed of a country that they could truly be proud of and for every Nigerian who has hoped for a bright new day in their beloved homeland where dreams are possible and aspirations are fulfilled, are the most sensible and most realistic solutions to Nigeria's problems ever proposed!

CONTENTS

REFORM IMPERATIVES FOR A NEW AND SUSTAINABLE NIGERIA

Nigeria, without question, is mired in many serious problems which threaten its very existence.

The biggest and perhaps the most crucial of Nigeria's problems is that Nigerians generally have no sense of country. This is why they treat their country like no-man's land fit only to take from and not to give to.

The notion that Nigeria is a no-man's land has also infused a winner-take-all mentality in the body politics of Nigeria and made political office a gateway to thievery and banditry.

Secondly, the federal system and structures Nigeria's current democracy is hoisted on is a military creation that was designed, shaped, and tailored to comport to military-style authoritarian dictatorship. This is why political leaders in Nigeria behave like overlords and tin-gods rather than the representatives of the people.

The federal system in Nigeria today is akin to wearing the right shoe on the wrong foot or wearing a dress the wrong side out.

Until we step back and rethink and create a system that is best suited for our twenty-first century clime, the journey to renewing and sustaining Nigeria as one country will be painful if not foolhardy.

Thirdly, governance in Nigeria is the exclusive preserve of the wealthy elite. The ordinary people in Nigeria are not involved and do not have a say in how their country is run. Politicians are loyal and accountable to political party machineries and not to the people. Nigeria's democracy is a huge scam for the unfettered exploitation of the country's wealth and economic repression of the ordinary people.

Any meaningful effort at reforming Nigeria must, without exception, address the following reform imperatives:

REDO OF THE CONSTITUTION

The 1999 Nigerian constitution upon which Nigeria's democracy is erected is a sham document riddled with many inconsistencies and redundancies. We have to scrap the current constitution and draw up one that is based strictly on Nigeria-style federalism tailored to Nigeria's socio-economic and ethno-cultural realities.

The so-called constitutional amendments of 2010 are insignificant and do not address the fundamental issues facing Nigeria. The amendments are mere cosmetic embellishments tailored by the political elite to consolidate their stranglehold on the reins of power in Nigeria.

RULE OF LAW/COURT SYSTEM

The current court/legal system in Nigeria does not guarantee that the rights of Nigerians are adequately protected. We have to revisit the system and install one that best guarantees the supremacy of the rule of law in Nigeria.

GOVERNANCE/POWERS

The federal system in operation in Nigeria is an authoritarian scam. We have to whittle down considerably the authoritarian powers of the federal government and install a system that ensures appropriate distribution of powers between the states, local governments and the federal government. The states under the new dispensation must be capable of exercising a level of autonomy that guarantees that they can thrive on their own and pursue interests closer to those of the people in their domains. This would have the effect of empowering the ethnic groups in their ethnic centers and de-emphasize competing ethnic interests at the federal level.

THE FOURTH TIER

Government and governance in the current dispensation are too far removed from the ordinary people of Nigeria. A vibrant and successful democracy in Nigeria depends on the participation of grassroots citizens in every nook and cranny of the country. We have to establish a fourth tier of government with administrative powers at the village or autonomous community level to bring governance closer to the people in order to ensure greater access to government resources and better accountability of common resources and public office.

NATIONAL RESOURCE

The current method of resource sharing in Nigeria is unfair and does not effectively compensate the people who directly bear the brunt of resource production. We have to install a system that ensures that while the federal government maintains control and regulation of oil and other natural resources, persons rather than communities enjoy first priority of consideration and are entitled to a percentage of earnings attributable to their appropriated land or facility.

ELECTORAL REFORMS

The so-called 2010 electoral reform touted by the political leadership in Nigeria is a mere cosmetic do-over that will continue to guarantee electoral fraud and undermine the integrity of elections. Real and drastic reforms must be instituted for real democracy to take root in Nigeria. Conduct of elections should be the exclusive preserve of local, municipal and village administrations. The national government has no business in conducting or overseeing the conduct of elections.

INFRASTRUCTURE

Control and regulation of infrastructure projects should remain the preserve of government but private sector participation and investment needs to be encouraged in areas of electricity generation and supply with government's role strictly limited to regulation and oversight. There is a need for massive and comprehensive overhaul of the infrastructure system in Nigeria with a refocus on large scale investments in modern infrastructure and a sound technological base that would propel Nigeria's economy from a wholly import dependent economy to a significant manufacturing/export economy.

PUBLIC SERVICE

The present public service system encourages corruption and inefficiency. We have to scrap the federal character reflecting system of balancing employment of public officials and institute a system based on qualification, experience and performance. The focus must be on an effective and efficient government and not on government of competing ethnic interests.

ECONOMY/EDUCATION/TECHNOLOGY

The economic future of Nigeria is bleak as the country continues to depend more and more on imported goods. Massive investments should be made in education and technology so that young people would be better equipped to meet the challenges of the future and through technological innovations help wean Nigeria off reliance on oil as the mainstay of its economy.

AN APPROACH TO SOLVING NIGERIA'S PROBLEMS

Bene diagnoscitur, bene curator

THERE IS A POPULAR BUT rarely applied aphorism that the first step to solving a problem is to understand the problem.

Understanding a problem involves not only deconstructing the genesis and character of the problem but also a deep and clear appreciation of its sundry parts and mechanics.

Understanding a problem is neither equivalent to knowing that the problem exists nor what the problem is. It does not begin and end with finding out what brought about the problem or unraveling what impact the problem has.

Understanding a problem affords the problem solver a clear and broad perspective of the problem solving options available and allows him or her to make the best and most-informed choice about which solutions will work.

Because only very few problem solvers approach problems as

they should, many of the world's problems remain unsolved and many of the ugly situations engendered by these problems remain festering.

This is especially true about Nigeria where just about all of the approaches to problem solving have begun with anything but taking the crucial first step of understanding just what is wrong with the country.

This is evident in the many failed efforts or lack of efforts to address the country's problems since it became independent of colonial rule in 1960.

For instance, the recent so-called constitutional amendments rather than addressing significant and fundamental issues in the constitution that will radically change the unsavory course of things in Nigeria merely addressed mundane and cosmetic issues.

Why did the political elite who are thumping their chests with pride for the so-called amendments suppose that by granting the national electoral commission financial autonomy it will become truly independent and electoral fraud will be a thing of the past?

As another example, why should we still be talking about religious riots and boundary disputes in Nigeria in the twenty-first century?

It is a disheartening and pathetic reality that these problems have existed in Nigeria for many decades and no serious efforts have been made to solve them and prevent the loss of thousands of innocent lives that occur every year.

The purpose of this book therefore is to put Nigeria's problems in an eye opening perspective, to better understand these problems and to proffer commonsensical, practical and realistic solutions that would set the country on a path to redemption and help forge a new beginning for the teeming millions of people who call the country their own.

The proffered solutions in the book are premised on the Latin refrain, *Bene diagnoscitur, bene curator;* meaning that a condition that is well diagnosed can be well cured.

The book is inspired by a growing concern that Nigeria's numerous problems have escalated to the point that they will very soon leave Nigerians without a country they could call their own.

It is similarly inspired by a profound faith and belief that Nigeria can still be fixed. That no matter how bad and intractable Nigeria's woes have become, the country can still be salvaged.

There is a reason why corruption and crime and social and moral decay are ubiquitous in Nigeria and there is a reason why they appear insurmountable.

There is a reason why in a country which produces the kind of wealth which would make many countries of the world green with envy, millions of people live in extreme conditions of poverty and deprivation.

There is a reason why a person who ascends to political office in Nigeria has only one purpose in mind; to loot public coffers.

There is a reason why a person who is fortunate to have a civil service job in Nigeria sees it as an opportunity to perpetuate a tradition that ensures that no public good can come from his effort.

There is a reason why the law enforcement personnel in Nigeria would rather look the other way while the most heinous of criminal activity is occurring under his nose.

There is a reason why a military or ex-military brass in Nigeria could flagrantly and wantonly abuse and brutalize an ordinary citizen and no one would dare take him to task.

There is a reason why many Nigerians have lost faith in the salvation of their country and have given up all hope that they would ever have a country they could be proud of.

And there is a reason why many people who could have tried to do something are discouraged from even trying and have become disinterested in any effort aimed at solving Nigeria's burgeoning problems.

In setting our sights at reforms in Nigeria, we should be able to take actions that would cause us at the end of the day to feel confident that our country has been renewed and that its future looks promising.

The book is Nigeria unraveled. It succinctly articulates the real problems with Nigeria and proffers well reasoned and practical ways about how the country can be made to work for all of its citizens.

As Nigeria takes one more turn into another political season, the book is intended as a roadmap for how the country can be reformed.

The book consists of four parts. Part A deconstructs and lays bare the root of Nigeria's problems and provides a unique multi-metrical and analytical perspective of how they have tracked Nigeria from its beginnings until this day.

Part B provides carefully articulated solutions to Nigeria's problems; from constitutional and electoral reforms to rule of law and infrastructure.

Part C explores the methods by which the solutions could be actualized considering that as a matter of conventional wisdom, change, especially change that threatens to upturn the cart of the status quo, will be aggressively resisted by those who will benefit if the status quo remains intact.

Part D consists of letters to selected Nigerians and reminds everyone of them of the need to become part of a collective drive to bring about the much-needed change in Nigeria.

The book is intended as a mirror of self and purpose re-evaluation for the teeming multitudes of politicians who have readied themselves once more for another season of unrestrained free-wheeling and barefaced thievery in Nigeria.

It is a reminder to Nigerians everywhere that we can no longer afford to be part and parcel of the stench and vile that our dear nation has become either by our inaction or by our active participation. That the more we sit or stand by while it is further subjected to irreparable despoliation by conmen and bandits in government and a moral fiber that has been worn thin by corrosive behavior, the more we stand to lose a country we all can call home.

It is a wakeup call to Nigerians of every stride and stripe no matter where they may be that we cannot keep hoping that one day Nigeria will be magically transformed through an act of God because no where else in the world has building a prosperous country depended entirely on God.

It is a wakeup call to Nigerians of every stride and stripe no matter where they may be that we cannot keep hoping that one day those in positions of power and influence will willingly institute the kind of transformation that our dear country direly needs because no where else in the world has powerful and influential people willingly surrendered their powers and influence and become disciples of the kind of change that would benefit ordinary people.

Love it or hate it, we have no other country but Nigeria. It is therefore our collective responsibility to ensure that Nigeria rises from a mediocre existence to become an efficient and truly egalitarian community that works for the good of every one of its citizens.

This is a rallying call to all progressive-minded Nigerians and it is a call to every Nigerian irrespective of ethnicity and religious creed and the only choice available is to be part of the solution and not part of the problem for no matter how long we dilly dally and procrastinate and no matter how much disappointed and disaffected we have become, change is very possible in Nigeria.

PART I

DECONSTRUCTING NIGERIA'S PROBLEMS

CHAPTER ONE

WHY NIGERIA NEEDS FIXING

It takes courage to solve a problem and cowardice to bestride it

NIGERIA NEEDS FIXING BECAUSE IT is not working for all Nigerians; it is working for only a handful of Nigerians.

Despite the social, economic and political gains many falsely believe the country has made in the last decade or so, Nigeria is a broken system that is built on false premises of democratic sustainability, economic viability and ethnic unity.

Nigeria needs fixing because it is not working for an overwhelming majority of its citizens who have been left out of the thievery and profligacy that have plagued the country since its independence fifty years ago.

Nigeria needs fixing because it has only worked out well for a tiny handful of well-connected and privileged people as well as their fortunate cronies, relatives and friends who have at various times managed to install themselves in the corridors of power and have corralled the proceeds from our collective resources for their personal purposes.

Nigeria needs urgent fixing because going by the way things have gone in the last decade, the country remains a fragile and delicate patchwork of sundry ethnic parts that have increasingly shown disinterestedness in coexisting with one another in order to forge a common front for collective sustainability.

Nigeria needs fixing because despite the billions of dollars it has earned from oil resources over the last fifty years, the country has very little to show for it and has not produced the kinds of results that are commensurate with its massive earnings especially in the areas of infrastructure, basic amenities and technology as well as human development and improvement.

Whether Nigeria has serious, wide-ranging problems that require urgent, drastic, and lasting solutions and how serious these problems are depends on the status perch of the Nigerian proffering an answer.

For the politician who has succeeded in planting one foot or two feet in the corridors of political power in the country and considers himself or herself privileged and positioned to share in the spoils of political office, Nigeria's problems may not be as bad as people make them out to be.

For many higher-ups in the political scale who line their pockets with the country's wealth at the expense of ordinary folks, things in Nigeria may not even be bad at all.

For a plenitude of political stalwarts and party officials and their top-echelon supporters who have benefited tremendously just because things are the way they are, Nigeria may not even have problems to begin with.

For the party insider or power broker who dictates the way

things are in Nigeria, the situation in Nigeria is not much different from the situation in the so-called first-world countries where democracy has been practiced for generations.

For the corrupt officials who pervade every sector of Nigeria and whose bread and butter depend entirely on a perverse status quo, any implying of problems within the system is deemed outrageous and any suggestion of change stands to be vehemently opposed.

For those who profit directly and indirectly from the spoils of a corrupt and inefficient system, the country has never been better than it presently is.

For the ex-military brass who enjoyed decades of plunder and pillage while in power and who has continued to maintain a stranglehold on the reins of power, Nigeria's milk of opportunity is ceaseless in its flow even if it flows for the benefit of a few.

For the ordinary Nigerian in the street who has toiled all his life to make the proverbial ends meet and has watched the wealth of his country squandered by a few well-placed people, Nigeria stinks to high heavens of every kind of problem.

For many Nigerians, especially those who have been victimized, the problem with Nigeria is crime.

For many more, it is economic and political corruption.

For most, it is lack of every thing from forthright leadership to even the most basic of amenities.

And for a great majority, it is moral and social decay.

For an overwhelming proportion of Nigerians who feel the pinch and pain of survival daily and who have been deprived and denied basic privileges and have endured severe hardship while their erstwhile neighbor who has made it into political office lavishes and splurges on the nation's wealth, it is hunger and starvation and the kind of poverty that makes them question the essence of their own existence.

For many Nigerians who have been tortured by the painful quagmires of a once-promising homeland and have labored in vain to salvage it from the doldrums, the problem is all of the above.

Nigeria needs fixing because the path it is threading is a one-directional track that would lead it to self-destruction.

There is no justifiable excuse why politics in Nigeria should be based on a winner-take-all mentality where people who find themselves in power freely flaunt their position and authority without any check or restraint whatsoever.

There is no justifiable excuse why the president should have such enormous and obscene powers as to be the sole controller of the nation's vast oil resources.

There is no justifiable excuse why a state governor in Nigeria could wield such enormous powers as to be beyond reproach by the other arms of government.

There is no justifiable excuse why the president is out of commission and there is an argument as to whether the vice president should fill in for him.

There is no justifiable excuse why the people cannot have faith in their power to vote when their votes will not count.

There is no justifiable excuse why Nigerians should tolerate a situation where politicians who live in their midst brazenly steal from public coffers and people just sit there and rue about it.

There is no justifiable excuse why ordinary Nigerians permit politicians who are supposed to serve them to behave like overlords and tin gods without raising uproars and hell for them.

To be sure, the problem is not that Nigerians do not know what the troubles with their country are; the problem is that they have become too accepting of and complacent about the country's problems.

The problem with fixing Nigeria is that those who have at various times attempted to solve its problems have not taken the crucial step to understand the nature and enormity and character of these problems.

Indeed, there have been many efforts and many attempts at tackling the many malaises that dog Nigeria but each has tended to bestride the real solutions that would bring real and lasting change.

For instance, most Nigerians believe that the best way to deal with the problem of corruption in Nigeria is to hound corrupt people into prison and to recapture stolen treasures from them.

Most Nigerians believe that the problem of crime in Nigeria can be addressed with simply equipping the Nigerian police with modern gadgets and super hi-tech paraphernalia.

Sadly, most Nigerians actually have the improvident belief that if they prayed hard and steadfast to God, God would make the country better.

As an example, because of the lack-luster performance of the national team at the 2010 soccer World Cup in South Africa, the government decided that the best way to make the team better was to ban it from international competitions for two years.

Would it not have been more expedient to find ways to better prepare next time and to actually do the things that would make the team better. Maybe building a more vibrant local league system as a means of cultivating, developing and enhancing talents would have been a far more sensible approach.

Another significant example is in the area of border disputes. Why should one community in Nigeria be at loggerheads with another about the demarcation lines between them when there should have been actual, documented and recorded demarcation lines when they were created that can be called up to resolve the dispute?

In one instance in the south-east of Nigeria, specifically the neighboring states of Abia and Akwa-Ibom, the federal government intervened in the boundary line dispute between two communities by erecting a military facility in the disputed area.

Would it not have been more expedient to pull up the original boundary lines that were drawn when the two states were created?

Or were there no surveys or territorial boundaries maps made when the states were created? Were the original boundary lines artificial? Or did no one think it fit to have them documented on paper at least?

These kinds of knee-jerk, hastily-contrived, and irascible problem solving techniques are emblematic of the many efforts to solve Nigeria's problems.

To be sure, many of the problems that exist in Nigeria such as pervasive corruption and high rates of crime are not peculiar to Nigeria. They exist elsewhere, even in developed countries as many Nigerian politicians would quickly point out.

However, there is uniqueness in the character and style and existential modes of these problems in Nigeria and that is what makes the huge difference.

The point here is not to treat the problems of corruption and crime and all the other problems that Nigeria is ridden with as strictly a Nigerian thing but to focus on how they have evolved and how they can be effectively curbed within the Nigerian context.

The task of fixing Nigeria is an onerous task that will require great courage and unwavering persistence. It is a task that must be pursued with resolve and will amount to hitting the reset button and starting all over with a clear and distinct idea of exactly what the country would be like at the end of the day.

The problems that dog Nigeria cannot be confronted and corrected with a patient, slow, ineffective, one-step-forward, three-steps-backward, leave-it-to-politicians, piecemeal approach which is very popular with the country's political elite.

The solutions must be wide reaching and wide ranging, comprehensive and sweeping and would touch on every aspect of Nigeria because every aspect is interconnected and every aspect is in decay.

For any meaningful change to happen in Nigeria, it has to be revolutionary, well articulated, and brought about by the action of ordinary people who have been denied the benefits of nationhood for far too long and have suffered the brutal consequences of a dysfunctional system.

Change in Nigeria must therefore be, as they say, from the bottom up and not from the top down.

History has shown that the people at the top have no incentives to bring about any meaningful change because one way or another, they benefit from the status quo and from systemic rot.

Because the ordinary people in Nigeria have been shortchanged for far too long, they must propel the engine of the kind of change Nigeria needs in order to achieve a sustainable and truly dynamic and progressive nation.

The challenge of people-driven reforms in Nigeria is enormous because majority of Nigerians are bereft of any kind of energy or incentive to resist the temptations of a corrupt system.

Most Nigerians have so much come to terms with the status

quo and have settled comfortably into the notion that there is a Nigerian way of doing things that is entirely Nigerian, that they would have to be coaxed into a new way of thinking in order for them to adapt to change.

The ordinary man in Nigeria sees himself as part and parcel of a corrupt system from which he stands to gain when his own time comes even when he is not certain that that time will ever come.

Most Nigerians have become reticent and accepting of corruption in their country and are willing participants in the decay because it has become the only way to get things done.

However, many Nigerians agree that there is something inherently wrong with the system and have only embraced the status quo because there are no other options available. In Nigeria, to not benefit from corruption is to be scorned and scoffed at.

The process of people-driven reforms in Nigeria therefore will have to be heralded by a massive reorientation and reeducation process that would center on proper messaging and commonsensical solutions that can easily be understood by the ordinary person in the street.

Ultimately, there is comfort and encouragement in the fact that most Nigerians are open-minded about change and will readily embrace one that makes sense and is realistic to them.

There is ample evidence suggesting that if the Nigerian is prodded, he is willing to do the right thing. Because of this, there is hope for change in Nigeria.

For any meaningful change to happen in Nigeria, it must be sensible, sustainable, realistic, realizable and practical and must take into consideration a multitude of factors.

The most crucial of these factors is the fact that Nigeria is a nation of 250 or more ethnic sub-nationalities each with its succinct and distinct ethnocentrism and unique socio-cultural and political perceptions.

Nigeria's body polity has so far ignored the fact that Nigeria is only not a homogeneous society but that our joining together as a nation was not voluntary and agreeable.

The idea is not to overemphasize Nigeria's ethnic differences and to trump up the fact that it is a country of unwilling and self-promoting and self-indulging ethno-centers, it is to understand that these factors have enduring implications for the country's continued existence and progress.

There have been many suggested ways to deal with Nigeria's problems and each reflects a myriad of sentiments that are out there.

Many are extreme and unpropitious. Many are based on principles of fairness and justness which arguably can only be possible if every other factor is present and the world is perfect place. Some are simply outrageous and overly radical.

There is only one true path to the solution to Nigeria's problems. It is neither one that seeks to give advantage to one group over the other nor demean one and elevate the other, but one that takes into consideration and recognizes the practical realities and the peculiarities of each component ethnic nationality.

In fashioning a solution, we have to be sure that it is one that is practical and realizable. It does not have to be perfect but it has to be one that will work. Core emphasis should be on realistic, realizable, sustainable and practical.

In doing so, we must have it in mind that the purpose of an efficient and well organized society is not to put every person in equal footing, but to bring a greater good to a greater number of people.

We must also bear in mind that the purpose of any well-organized and efficient society is not to ensure that every member has the same amounts of gold and silver but that every member has a fair chance to thrive as much as his ability permits.

The ordinary Nigerian like ordinary people everywhere is not asking for too much. He is not crying because he does not live in an opulent mansion or that he does not drive around in a posh car or enjoy gourmet meals fit for kings and queens; he is crying because he has no viable roof over his head, has no reliable means of transporting himself and cannot afford a meal fit for even a rat.

The best the society can do for the ordinary person is to provide him with basic necessities that would make his already basal existence manageable. And that is the biggest reason why Nigeria needs fixing.

Chapter Two

THE REAL PROBLEM WITH NIGERIA

Unwittingly we invited the problem; willingly we succumbed to it

THE REAL PROBLEM WITH NIGERIA is not copious corruption or odious crime or decayed infrastructure or religious bigotry or mediocre mindset. Those are just the unfortunate byproducts of the real problem.

The real problem with Nigeria is that Nigerians have no sense of country, period.

Nigerians have no sense of country because Nigeria's socio-political core has been overwhelmed by a new kind of brazen ethnic and pseudo-ethnic competition which has engendered an atmosphere in which each Nigerian sees himself or herself more as part of a smaller ethnic unit than as part of a national whole.

Sadly, not many Nigerians in their actions and behavior and attitudes have shown that they care for a Nigeria that exists for the collective interests of all Nigerians.

Not many Nigerians have willingly come to terms with the fact that Nigeria is an indispensable reality and that the more we fan the embers of ethnic rivalry and divisiveness, the further we push the country closer to disintegration.

No, the issue here is neither whether Nigerians are patriotic nor whether they love their country. To love one's country and to be patriotic to one's country are far higher standards and very few Nigerians will pass that muster.

Indeed, one has to have a sense that he belongs to a country first before he can love it and before he can even be patriotic towards it.

All of Nigeria's problems are rooted in the fact that Nigerians have come to see their homeland as a no-man's or another man's land from which to pillage rather than to which to give.

There is no longer zeal to act in a national interest because national interest is anathema to Nigerians.

There is no longer commitment to national well-being because there is no true national common front.

There is no concerted effort to build a prosperous and successful nation because there is no mutually inclusive and collective destiny.

In short, Nigeria is now a jungle where every man schemes for himself, under the guise of ethnic preference and at the expense of the country.

For majority of Nigerians, the famous JFK exhortation; *"ask not what your country can do for you but what you can do for your country"* is an obnoxious notion that has no place whatsoever in the Nigerian context.

In fact, going by the way things have panned out in Nigeria for the past fifty years, there is no indication that there is a Nigerian, especially the Nigerian aspiring to political office, who sees political office as a platform for service and for contributing to a common good.

Each man or woman is in the race for what he can grab for himself or herself.

In Nigeria, elective office is not about service to country, it is about individual greed, personal aggrandizement and sustaining the winner-take-all mindset of the status quo.

At the core of this lack of sense of country is the fact that by design and in practice, Nigeria is fashioned as a country of ethnicities rather than a nation of individuals.

From the time the country's sundry parts were joined together in a delicate patchwork called amalgamation in 1914 up until this day, Nigeria's political, social, economic, and cultural structures have operated under the false notion that Nigeria is made up of monolithic and cohesive ethnic centers through which a collective or national agenda could be achieved while individually pursuing narrow ethnic interests.

Today, everywhere, rather than work for the common good of the nation, these ethnic centers have quadrupled in number and are poised to scheme only for what they can get from the country and not what they can contribute to it.

Today, the national arena in Nigeria is comprised of more than 250 ethnic groups and quasi-groups, each well-organized and well-armed with self-gratifying agenda, to outdo and out-possess one another.

Today, the national center stage consists of an endless tussle by competing ethnic interests scheming to achieve one thing and one thing only, seize control of the national purse.

While it was reasonable for Britain to conceive and then shape Nigeria as a nation of ethnic groups at the time Nigeria was put together, the concept has not panned out as being in the best interest of the country after all.

Because of this, most Nigerians see themselves first from the hyper-prism of ethnic identity before they see themselves as Nigerians. And in the end, the country suffers.

Although Britain instituted a framework that emphasized ethno-cultural differences in Nigeria when the country was created, it did so because it was the only choice open to it.

It made sense then because Britain was of the erroneous belief that each of the ethnic centers was a monolithic and cohesive ethnic platform that was both inclusive and exercised control over a wide geographic region and therefore could coalesce at the center for a common national good.

The concept of emphasizing ethnic identity worked for Nigeria for a good while especially in the thick of colonialism when there began a vibrant ethnic nationalism and consciousness which gave rise to the first hints of Nigerian nationalism. This would pave the way for Nigeria's independence.

Ethnic nationalism and ethnic consciousness and the fierce ethnocentrism they fostered also gave rise in the wee-years of colonialism to a healthy competition amongst the ethnic groups.

This in turn prompted a dramatic development drive within the ethnicities and instigated a race between the ethnic groups to an imaginary finish line at which each hoped to proclaim victory.

The inter-ethnic competitive spirit then was healthy and well-intentioned because it awakened Nigeria's ethnic subparts to a need to self-develop and to better position them to be considered equal partners in a sovereign cause and to be equal stakeholders in the national arena.

By the 1930s and 1940s, many of the slow-starter ethnic groups had measurably closed the gap and in many respects were at par with their competitors and counterparts from other ethnicities.

By the late 1950s when Nigerian nationalism had reached its full fervor and the colonial power of Britain had waned considerably, the inter-ethnic competition especially amongst the so-called three major ethnic groups within which a multitude of subparts were subsumed, had reached a troubling peak as each retuned and sharpened their nationalistic verve for a new kind of struggle.

At the dawn of 1960 as Nigeria turned the final bend on the road to independence, it was already clear that there was a full-fisted rivalry amongst the ethnic groups to gain control of the emerging national stage.

The once-healthy competition that melded into a nationalistic zeal had become soured and explosive as the common enemy in Britain began the process of relinquishing control.

By the time Britain finally departed and hoisted a fledgling democracy on the shoulders of the once-fraternally united Argonauts of the struggle for independence, the stage was effectively set for a catastrophic showdown with lasting implications.

With the common foe gone, it was inevitable that a new enemy would have to be found and Nigerians found that enemy amongst themselves.

Inter-ethnic competition turned into inter-ethnic rivalry and the struggle for a collective national interest transmogrified into an ethnocentric selfish purpose. And thus, the country was set on a permanent path to self-destruction.

Of course, this concept was not peculiar to Nigeria. Across the African continent and in other parts of the world in which colonial powers emphasized ethnic demarcations and differences similar scenarios have played out.

Indeed a cursory appraisal of the concept shows that in almost all of the countries of the world which have witnessed and continue to witness decades of instability, political tussles, social decay and corruption, armed violence and economic stagnation, the major contentious issues have been couched on ethnic differences.

It is not at all surprising therefore that in most of the so-called developed world political differences are based on political ideology and philosophy while in most of the so-called developing world political differences are based on ethnic predilection and ethno-cultural agenda.

What has happened from the time of Nigeria's independence in 1960 until this day is an expansion and multiplication of the notion of ethnic nationalism with the gradual dilution of the three former major ethnic blocs.

Today, we no longer speak in terms of power sharing or economic distribution between three major ethnic groups, we are now dealing with more than 250 distinct ethnic fronts.

In essence, Nigeria is confronted today with more than 250 times the situation it faced in the immediate post-independence period and that is the root of Nigeria's present-day troubles.

In a nutshell, when three major ethnicities sworn to rivalry against one another were at the fore of things in Nigeria in the 1960s, their rivalries produced a disgorgement of the remaining sense of collective national interest, heralded a massive spate of corruption, instigated the first ever military coup, spawned a bitter civil war which decisively dismembered whatever was left of a national common core and corroded whatever vestiges of inter-ethnic trust and cooperation left.

Here in the twenty-first century we have 250 competing interests and the prize is still the same.

The massively troubling problem therefore is how to harmonize these competing interests and still maintain a cohesive country.

While it used to be three major rivals squabbling on the national stage to take the reins of power in Nigeria, today, there are 250 rivals and they have all come well-armed and sensitized for a no-holds-barred showdown.

While it was easier in the years prior to the current political dispensation which began in 1999 to work the interests of three major ethnic blocs into the national fabric through notions of power sharing, federal character reflecting and quota systems, it is an onerous challenge to attempt to do so now with 250 distinct ethnic interests.

There, enmeshed within that challenge is the core of Nigeria's problems.

The point here is not that the smaller ethnic groups who have been awakened from their complacence have no right to demand their place in the national scheme of things in Nigeria. It is however that it was inevitable and took a long time to manifest.

For far too long we defined the character and tenor of Nigeria's socio-political clime in terms of three major ethnic groups and glossed over the existence of small ethnic groups with simplistic classifications that tended to benefit some Nigerians and not all Nigerians.

For far too long, we have gotten away with relegating some Nigerians to the background because of the size of their ethnic group while the major ethnic blocs basked in the sunshine of political and economic advantage.

Now that the small ethnic *giants* have awakened and are

demanding their stake in the national arena, we cannot continue to dwell on old definitions and irrational classifications.

Now is the time to redefine Nigeria's character because there is simply no feasible mathematical formula for working 250 ethnic identities into an effective system of power sharing, federal character reflecting or quota distribution.

To attempt to do so will be calamitous and to pretend that the problem does not exist will only leave us with a Nigeria that is not worthy to be called a country.

For Nigeria to be truly viable as a country, the only choice open to us is to summon the will and the courage to redefine our country as a nation of individuals rather than as a nation of ethnicities.

In redefining our country, we will not only be developing a template worthy of emulation by other nations especially in Africa which are similarly ensconced in insurmountable woes, we will be unshackling our nation from the truly destabilizing and detrimental legacies and mindsets bestowed upon us by colonialism for ever.

CHAPTER THREE

HOW ETHNICITY DEFINES NIGERIA'S CHARACTER

I am an individual before I am a member of an ethnic group before I am a citizen of a country

NIGERIA AS MANY WOULD PREFER to think of it is neither an aberration nor a mishap. It is the handiwork of Britain, a colonial master whose only objective in the dark days of colonialism was to maintain its self-serving interests in the African continent.

Nigeria was thus a creation of opportunity and necessity. It was not formed by compromise. The 250 plus ethnic nationalities that inhabit the country today did not come to a table to form a union. They were neither agreeable nor willingly submissive to being mashed together.

In reality though, not many countries of the world were formed willingly or by agreement or as a matter of compromise between its sundry parts.

The notion therefore that people have to be a willing part

of a whole before harmony and progress can be achieved is misguided.

The simple fact is that most successful countries have been successful because there were people of foresight who were willing to make the most out of their given situation.

What happened in Nigeria in 1914 under the auspices of Lord Lugard the British overlord in the region at that time was an expansion of the opportunistic pursuits of a colonial power desperate to maintain effective control over a cohesive geographic entity in order to better milk its resources.

Thus, Lord Luggard's priority was not whether the mash-up will sustain; rather it was whether it would make for more effective management.

Here in the 21st century many Nigerians are still quibbling about whether the amalgamation was the proper thing to do and whether their country was meant to be.

Many are still struggling to gulp down the bitter truth that even if there were many flaws in the amalgamation process, Nigeria was a viable political entity when it was created.

At the heart of Nigeria's many intractable problems is the fact that in the minds of many Nigerians, accepting the undoable reality that Nigeria is here to stay has proved difficult and this manifests not only in their pronouncements but also in the way most Nigerians treat their country.

Whether Nigerians like it or not, the country is here to stay and the sooner that fact is reflected in deeds and in spirit, the sooner we would all work in concert to raise the country from the doldrums of economic and political rot and begin the arduous task of building a nation of which every Nigerian would be truly proud.

If the amalgamation of 1914 was a mistake, it has already been made.

If it was ill-informed, it is too late to undo.

We have no choice now.

We have no other country but Nigeria.

Whether we like it or not, Nigeria is one indivisible country consisting of 250 plus ethnic nationalities carved up into 36 States.

There is nothing wrong with the geopolitical structure in place today because it puts us in the best position to harness our resources effectively and redefine our objectives in order to build a truly prosperous nation.

Any suggestion about going back in time to question the validity of the creation of the country in 1914 through the mechanism of a sovereign national conference as many distinguished Nigerians have suggested, is foolhardy and fruitless venture which would only re-ignite a sentiment of disintegration that should be well behind us.

It would definitely re-instigate an agitation for disgorgement and dismemberment which has plagued us till this day.

Any question about whether Nigeria is sustainable as one country is a recipe for disaster. We can only work with what providence has hefted unto our shoulders.

The real question is how to make what we have work for us while taking into consideration the peculiarities of our multi-ethnic component parts.

Against the projections of many contrary opinions, Nigeria is better off, more viable, and more sustainable as one country.

Also, Nigeria's present political system operates on a false assumption that the differences among its diverse ethnic parts are mere paper classifications that can we worked over by simplistic notions of quota distribution, rotational political office agreements and federal character-reflecting public sector appointments.

It is this false sense of power and resource sharing between imagined cohesive ethnic blocs that is at the heart of Nigeria's problems.

It has engendered a lack of sense of country and fostered a sense of self-centered individual pursuit rather than a patriotic sense of collective aspiration.

Any meaningful effort to reform Nigeria must therefore first address the issue of Nigeria's nationhood not by questioning the propriety of the amalgamation of 1914, not by rationalizing whether Nigeria should be one country of mutually agreeable partners, but by keying in the fact of the country's multi-ethnicity into the boilerplate of fashioning a socio-political system that works for every one of its ethnic groupings and by extension, every Nigerian.

The questions to ask and answer are; how do we redefine the prevalent sense of unwillingness within the various ethnic components to be part of a whole into a mutually-inclusive and agreeable sense of country?

How do we convert the pervading ethnocentrism into national patriotism?

How do we make our heterogeneity work for us rather than against us?

How do we redirect the me-first mentality of the average Nigerian that makes him see the country as a pillaging ground for self aggrandizement to a we-first mentality of collective aspiration and endeavor?

How do we convert the sense of self-opportunism in the political office holder to a sense of service for national good?

A realistic starting point for answering the foregoing questions is to debunk and disavow many of the assumptions and notions of ethnocentrism which have tended to divide and weaken rather than unite and strengthen.

For instance, there is a well-entrenched false notion that to thrive, each of the three major ethnic groups as well as the other two hundred and forty-seven or so minor ethnic centers must organize to scheme for their interests as a group.

There is an assumption that each group must of necessity articulate their respective demands and standpoints in order to secure their interest in the nation.

It has become fashionable these days to hear and see the agitations of progressive unions and ethnic associations from every nook and cranny of Nigeria, each positioned to gain an advantage in the national scheme of things, each demanding their fair shake in the national arena.

Whereas ethnic associations ought to primarily organize to promote intra-ethnic cultural and social causes, these days, it has become the only avenue by which members could realize personal economic sustenance and political relevance.

However, while many people speak in terms of ethnic agenda, beyond the projected notions of ethnic common-cause is the prioritization of individual pursuit firstly for the individual and his immediate family, secondly for his immediate community and thirdly for his ethnic identity.

In other words, a person is a person first before he is part of an ethnic group and before he is part of a nation.

The notion that there is or should be an Igbo common-agenda

or a Yoruba common-agenda or an Hausa-Fulani common-agenda or the common-agendas of other smaller ethnic or tribal classifications is a misnomer and is perhaps one of the biggest stumbling blocks to Nigeria's unity and sustainability.

It has tended to pit one ethnic group against the other in a perpetual struggle and demeaned any sense of national center.

It has dogged every sphere and stage of Nigeria's existence since Independence and has proven to be more of an exacerbating factor for disunity and mutual distrust.

The idea of ethnic agenda within the subparts presupposes that there is an adversarial national center with which each ethnic group must contend and against which each must wage a battle in order to ensure group survival.

Sadly, the nationalistic zeal and struggle of the colonial days when great Nigerians of every stripe banded together to wrest control of their country from a colonial power has transmogrified into an adversarial zeal defined by tribal affinity.

While colonialism lasted, it was easy to define a common enemy and to define a common cause. Nigerians were joined at the hip in their common quest for emancipation. However as soon as we chased the colonial common-foe out and tasted the forbidden fruit of independence, we turned around and found new enemies amongst our ranks.

From common friends with identical stakes, we became common enemies with divergent aspirations.

From sweetheart compatriots with mutual interests we became bitter rivalries scheming against one another.

Unfortunately, the feeling of inter-ethnic distrust and suspicion caused Nigeria's first failures as an infant nation and has persisted until this day.

Today, we are left with a scenario in which one ethnic group sees itself as an adversary of the other in a full-fisted contest to secure control of the national machinery.

Each ethnic group sees itself in competition with the other, aiming only to satisfy the yearning of its ethnocentric core thereby promoting a situation where ethnic predilection is paramount while the interests of the nation is secondary or inconsequential.

Today Nigeria as a nation is a no-man's-land of competing ethnic interests where people care more for personal and ethnic satisfaction rather than a national sense of pride.

While we dwell in the falsehood that we have forged a country of one people and one culture united for a common purpose, we are in reality a nation of many distinct peoples and many cultures each with its distinct objectives.

While we assume that we are a country of similar people with similar causes willing to uphold a common promise we are in reality a conglomerate of dissimilar people with divergent agendas willing to pursue personal or narrow group promise.

However, the notion of ethnic nationalism as propounded by the so-called ethnic unions and organizations in Nigeria and abroad is actually a farce.

Each ethnic association or progressive union with its grandiose agendas and rabble-dousing inflections has not particularly augured well for a great majority of the people within the ethnic group for whom they purport to organize.

Most have merely pursued narrow interests that benefit their elite classes of organizers and benefactors.

In other words, ethnic nationalism in Nigeria is a perverse pyramid scheme where only the people at the top echelons of the ethnic association enjoy the benefits of organizing.

In reality, ethnic affinity and the will to organize is strongest only when people are outside their ethnic enclaves. Each ethnic group appears like a monolithic entity on the national and international stages but within their ethnic enclaves, minor divisions and mini classifications quickly manifest and people immediately identify with sub groups.

Outside their ethnic enclaves, each association gives the impression that it is a formidable front for collective aspiration but back in their home turf their differences and sub-tribal divisions come to the fore.

For this reason, the ordinary people within each ethnic group feel left out of any supposedly common agenda.

In order words, when the organizers of an ethnic association claim that they are organizing so that they can bring goodies from the national coffers to their people they are only doing so as a front for personal promotion.

This is borne out by the fact that across Nigeria, none of these ethnic associations have attracted any real benefits to their people.

Rather, their helmsmen have received political appointments and contracts and have enriched themselves personally in the guise of lobbying for ethnic interests.

It is obvious that a Nigerian body politic that focuses on cohesive or monolithic ethnic fronts as the basis for individual aspiration without taking into consideration the reality that people are first and foremost individuals before they are part of an ethnic group has not worked and will never work for Nigeria.

In order to achieve a balanced and more just nation, the new focus must center on individual identity rather than on a false notion of ethnic groupings and collective common-fronts.

In essence, Nigeria must be redefined first and foremost as a nation of individuals before it considers itself as a nation of multiple ethnicities.

Again, a person is first and foremost an individual before he is a member of a group and before he is a member of a nation.

The notion that one should first and foremost figure out what part of Nigeria another comes from before he sees what he has to offer is misplaced and accounts for many of the foibles of Nigeria.

People should not be judged by their ethnic affiliation but by their individual worth.

The point ultimately is not to ignore the fact of Nigeria's ethnic variety, but to appreciate the fact that overplaying the hand of ethnicity divides more than it unites; it weakens more than it strengthens; it creates a condition of distrust rather than engender mutual tolerance, it promotes unhealthy rivalry rather than inspiring mutual coexistence.

For Nigeria to thrive, each individual within each ethnic group must be empowered and given an opportunity to pursue his life's ambitions to the fullest extent possible.

The best way to achieve this is to empower the individual's local community and create opportunities within the smallest ethnic community so that the individual will once more have a sense of belonging and worth first in his smaller tribal community, second in his larger ethnic affiliation and thirdly in his nation.

To summarize, Nigeria's biggest problem lies in the fact that not many Nigerians have any sense of country.

The lack of sense of country promotes a situation where most Nigerians see their country as a no man's land good only for taking from rather than giving to.

Unfortunately, most of the solutions that have been proffered about combating Nigeria's woes have tended to revolve around the concept of ethnic balancing which presupposes that the yearnings of each member of an ethnic group can be assuaged by appointing a person from his ethnicity to a political office in the hope that that alone will make him feel that he is relevant.

However, because of the culture of ethnic balancing there is a lack of interest in building a national common front and because there is a lack of interest in building a national common front, the teeming millions of ordinary Nigerians whose best hope lie in a truly prosperous nation suffer untold bitter consequences.

Whether we like it or not, we can no longer sustain a culture in which the national center feels that it has done enough for a person just because someone from his ethnic group has been appointed to an important political office.

We cannot continue a system that dwells on a foolhardy notion that the president of Nigeria must come from my ethnicity before I can feel at home in Nigeria or before I can love it and contribute to its improvement.

We cannot continue a system that gives a false impression that if the president of Nigeria comes from my ethnicity he would use his powers to bring goodies and economic and infrastructure benefits to me and my community and if a person from another ethnicity becomes president, my community would suffer neglect.

Why should I care who the president of Nigeria is and what ethnicity he or she comes from as long as I enjoy the full benefits and privileges of a stable and prosperous nation?

Why should I care what ethnicity the minister for works comes from when I have good roads to travel on and uninterrupted supply of electricity and water?

Why should I care what ethnicity the minister of education comes from when there is a sound education policy in place and good schools for my children to attend?

We certainly cannot continue a culture of winner-take-all in which a person takes political office and awards contracts only to his ilk and friends.

Why should it be up to one person to decide who gets contracts and who does not? Why should absolute power be reposed in one office and in one person that make securing control of that office a do-or-die affair?

Sadly, these notions are deeply entrenched in and have pervaded Nigeria's socio-political and economic landscapes since independence and unless something urgent and drastic is done we would have no country to call our own.

Chapter Four

HOW CORRUPTION ATE NIGERIA'S SOUL

It's here, there, and everywhere; it's you, me, and everyone. We accept and perfect it at the same time that we decry and inveigh it

CORRUPTION HAS BECOME SO INTEGRATED into Nigeria's national fabric and has eaten away every scintilla of decency in our social and cultural fiber that it is almost unthinkable that the scourge can ever be surmounted.

Nigerians of all stripes, not just politicians and public office holders are possessed and consumed by corruption to the extent that we have come to accept it as an integral part of who we are.

We have become so used to it as a way of life that we no longer find it obnoxious or shocking. Even the vilest form of it now has the sweet aroma of something expected and welcome.

Just to give you an idea, consider the following missives.

I was in Lagos not long ago and I lost my way in the giddiness of Obalende. I stopped to ask this little boy on the street for directions and much to my befuddlement, after pointing me in the right way, he pushed his palm in my face and said, "Oga you have to settle me."

He said it with such seriousness and alacrity that I was completely stupefied. "Settle you for what?" I queried my mouth agape in wonderment.

"Abi," he returned, maintaining his searing gaze at my eyeballs, "the direction wey I give you, you no need am? Abeg settle me joo."

Now I was thoroughly flabbergasted. I wished then that I could give him back what he just gave me so that I would be free of his menace. I also felt cowed and deflated.

"Why you no tell me say e go cost me something?" I demanded as I lamely fished in my wallet for a 100 Naira note.

"Befor nko? Abi you no know say na Nigeria we dey?" He retorted.

He took the 100 Naira and hissed as he skulked away and I could tell that he was not even impressed by the 100 Naira.

Then there was another time when I was unfortunate to have my car stuck in a crater-sized pot hole on a road in Lagos. I was immediately accosted by half-a-dozen youth who seemed to have been crouching out of sight nearby. Grinning ear to ear as if they had just netted a robust deal, they demanded I pay them some hefty amount to get my car out which I did. And when out of pretended naiveté I asked why the road was in such a bad shape, they scoffed at me and one said, "Haba oga, you be JJC? This na our own business center. If they fix am, we go spoil am. We no go gree them take our business from us." I got the point.

Then one time, I went to this palatial mansion in Lagos to see a so-called big man residing there. When I got to the huge gates, I was accosted by a uniformed guard who demanded to know my reason for coming.

"I want to see chief," I told him.

"Chief no dey," he returned tersely.

"But I called on the phone and he knows I'm coming," I said.

"Well, chief no tell me," he replied.

"Well go ask him," I pressed.

"Wetin you wan' see chief for?" he queried.

And my frustration grew. Luckily, "Chief" had another visitor who knew me and who had his way with the guard so I got in to see chief on the visitor's good grace.

On my way out, the guard sidled up to me. "Oga you go see me sha," he quipped, his tone clearly friendly now.

"I'm seeing you already with my eyeballs," I replied testily.

"Ah oga no vex. Jus' find me something," he insisted.

"Find you something for what?" I demanded.

"If no be me, you for no see oga. Na me open gate for you." He returned slyly.

He was an idiot, I could see. I left without another word. I'm betting I would have a tougher time if I ever went back.

Then check out this one about this poor chap who went to some ministry in Abuja to submit an application for employment.

The unassuming applicant did get beyond the gates and into an inner office where he warmly greeted a clerk and handed over his application. Then after a brief stop at another office to make inquiries he left to go home. Outside the gates he bought some groundnuts from a street vendor and discovered to his utter consternation that the paper with which his groundnuts were wrapped was the application he had just submitted.

Apparently he had neglected to "put something on top" of his application for the clerk when he submitted it and the application had followed him out the gates of the ministry rather than being forwarded for consideration.

These are just some examples of the decay in the mindset of most Nigerians. They are excoriating examples of why corruption has become Nigeria's first nature. It is not just in high places, it's in low places. It's everywhere, it involves all Nigerians.

In one fashion or the other, we breathe, live, eat, drink, and indulge corruption, every one of us. Well, maybe ninety-nine percent of Nigerians.

That's how bad it is.

Most people wrongly believe that the problem of corruption begins and ends in high places and with politicians and public office holders.

We all prefer to point fingers at others but not ourselves. We blame politicians, the police, public officials, and the military. We blame everyone else but ourselves. Even the corrupt politician points fingers at other corrupt politicians. We blame everyone else for corruption but ourselves even when we reek and stink and revel in it.

To be sure, corruption was not invented in Nigeria. However, we have taken it, embraced it, cuddled it and made it our own. We exist in it rather than it existing in us.

It hosts us rather us hosting it. It is our process of doing things rather than an item in the way we do things. It is usually excused with the popular refrain, "*this na Naija*".

Corruption is so ubiquitous in Nigeria that without it, you cannot get anything done.

You cannot buy something without paying an excess amount for it even if you are a savvy buyer.

And if you are not careful, you will buy a dress shirt from the market only to discover when you get home that it has no sleeves.

Or you will buy a can of sardines only to find out that the expiration date on the can has been scratched off or altered.

You cannot get employment even if you tout the best qualifications.

And if you do not grease someone's palm your credentials will not be considered.

Or someone else will use your credentials to get hired.

You cannot get government business or contract even if you have the most realistic bid or proposal.

And even if you have the best equipment around someone else will get the contract and pay you peanuts to do the work.

Or if you want you can take the money and not do the work.

You cannot even go to see your friend if he lives in a mansion and has a security person at his gate.

And if you are not vigilant, someone will demand something from you for saying "good morning" to you.

Or require you to pay him first before he can tell you "good afternoon".

You cannot buy something from the market, take it home, find it defective or change your mind and return it to the vendor for a refund.

Oh no, not on your life.

Where do you think you are?

Whatever you pay for, you have to keep it whether you like it or not.

You cannot hand over money for any reason for that matter and then turn around and ask for it back.

That would be an abomination and you will be scorned and reprimanded.

Corruption permeates every pore, every crack, every cranny, every nook, every callow, every camber, every confine, every crevice, and every cell of Nigeria's existence.

In short, Nigeria is now officially a *Corruptocracy* (government of corruption, by corruption, and for corruption or Government of corrupt people, by corrupt people, for corrupt people).

Corruption is implicit in every contract, every deal, every transaction, every conversation, every discussion, every scheme, every appointment, every negotiation, every position, every office, every edifice, and every structure.

In theory and in practice, corruption no longer exists in Nigeria rather Nigeria exists in corruption. Corruption is the iceberg; Nigeria is now only the tip.

Corruption has eaten and imbibed the remnants of the Nigerian soul to the extent that most Nigerians, big and small, old and young, rich and poor are now bereft of any conscience.

Corruption is now not only the exclusive preserve of the policeman and the political office holder; it is the little boy who wants something in return for helping an old folk cross the street.

It is the market vendor who would sell you a shirt with only a front side but packaged to look like it is a complete shirt.

It is the seller of goods who would swear that the goods he is selling to you is the real stuff when he knows that it is a fake.

It is still the school boy who would lie to his uneducated

parents that he needs to buy a packet of photosynthesis for science class.

It is the self-appointed pastor or self-nominated man of God who would encourage you to keep the loot you have carted from government coffers and to see it as God's blessing as long as you give him ten percent of the loot.

It is the school teacher who brings stuff to sell to other teachers in school rather than sit in class and teach.

It is the Nigerian no matter where you will find him or her.

Whatever is left of the country is in the throes and thralls of sure demise because of corruption but no one seems to notice or even care.

Nigerians now suffer from compulsive and spontaneous corruption to the extent that we can no longer restrain ourselves.

Even those who profess a religious faith are smack in the midst and middle of corruption.

It is no longer sin or thievery.

It is no longer something to be ashamed of.

It is now something to boast of.

And be proud of.

And celebrate.

It is now so much the norm that one can guarantee that even those who steal from government coffers do not fully appreciate the fact that they could be doing something terrible.

They pillage our treasures as a matter of entitlement and of right. That's how come they see nothing untoward in their actions.

Said one politician, "If I don't steal, somebody else will."

So he is merely beating the next bandit to the loot.

The national treasure is no longer for a common purpose; it is now for the first to get there.

First come, first served.

For him or her, there cannot be anything wrong with taking for himself or herself the treasure that belongs to all.

And if he has the opportunity to steal and he does not utilize it, he would be a laughing stock of others.

If you are not corrupt, you are a bloody fool.

And no one should have given you an important office in the first place.

That's how much Nigeria has embraced corruption.

Indeed, all Nigerians are victims of an enemy that they invited in their home and gave the impetus to destroy their country.

Every Nigerian, even the Nigerian who wears corruption as a vest is a victim.

We are all victims because we have permitted to stand systems and structures that make it easy for corruption to thrive.

We have erected a national storehouse of treasures and we have continuously entrusted the keys to just one person to control and manage it as he sees fit. If he be not corrupt at the time of the entrusting, mightn't we have neglected the fact that he is human and temptation is no respecter of humans?

I am always amazed when people express consternation at a report that some political office holder has absconded with millions of dollars or billions of naira.

"Can you imagine that?" They would say in bewilderment and anger.

"Yes I can." I would retort with a knowing smile.

What do they expect?

When the system places so much authority at the hands of

one person to the extent that the president of Nigeria has the only say-so on every contract and every oil deal in Nigeria, why should anyone be surprised that with a stroke of the pen he could steal every dime the country has and have the guts to laugh in our faces.

When there is no effective system of checks and balances and the minister or governor or local government chairperson, or counselor, or commissioner behaves as if his office is a personal investment what you have is a conscienceless society that breeds and encourages criminal behavior.

When there is no effective system of accountability in which a winner-take all mentality is prevalent, what you have is a despoiled community in which people are not expected to be forthright.

When it is easy for the police to take extra-judicial action by locking a person in jail just because another person has given them money to do so, what you have is a perverse society where abuse of power and authority reigns supreme.

When you have a system in which a crime victim pays the police for the upkeep of the victimizer or suspect in jail and for investigation of the crime as well as transportation of the suspect to court, what you have is a bastardization of the notion of justice.

When you have a judicial system in which a case in court has to be put on hold because the judge or magistrate is away for a few months on a personal matter, what you have is a derelict judicial process in which people are forced to resort to self-remedies.

When you have a system in which the ordinary man has no basic knowledge of his fundamental rights guaranteed by the constitution and those in the know exploit his ignorance, what you have is a nation which does not offer any form of protection for the ordinary citizen.

When you have a system in which people act with impunity and without fear of repercussions, what you have is a country that is sure to fail.

I agree with former President Obasanjo when he suggested that the systems and structures in place in Nigeria are so wantonly derelict and decayed that even if Jesus Christ himself came down to conduct elections in Nigeria, they cannot be free and fair.

Indeed how can elections in Nigeria be free and fair when we still rely on election officials to be sincere and true to their service to their fellow Nigerians? How can elections be fair when by their very nature, Nigerians are corrupt? Why should anyone expect a corrupt system to produce honest results?

I agree with all those Nigerians who have thrown their arms in defeat and frustration and are quick to quip that Nigeria is unsalvageable from the hands of odious corruption.

I agree more with all those Nigerians who say that we must do something about corruption in Nigeria.

I agree with many Nigerians who say that public office holders and politicians must be taken to task and held accountable.

However in setting our sights on righting the wrongs of our country, I do not agree that we should busy ourselves chasing after people and their stolen wealth.

Rather I am for ensuring that it never happens again.

No matter how much we rail about the things that have already gone awry, it is still foolhardy and unproductive to cry over spilt milk.

We must let bygones be bygones. The past can only serve as a teachable history of the paths we should avoid and cannot afford to thread. We must be forward looking.

That's a more practical and realistic approach.

If the money was stolen, it was not properly safeguarded.

If people are corrupt, it is because the system encourages and allows it.

If I see a thief running from my house with a bag of loot, I will not waste my time chasing after him especially when I may never catch up with him. I would go to my house to investigate how it is that the thief was able to get in. I would then reinforce the security in my house so that when the thief or his ilk returned he or they would not be able to gain entrance again.

That is the realistic and practical way to combat the scourge of Corruption in Nigeria.

No matter how rotten and broken the system in Nigeria has become, it is fixable.

Nigeria's best bet is to embark on sweeping and comprehensive reforms that would re-kit and retool and restructure and redefine the systems and structures in place so that no one Nigerian will ever be in a position to control our destiny and to avail himself of our national treasure.

Whatever changes we need to make would have to be revolutionary. There would be resistance because change is a bitter pill.

We would need a lot of will power and resolve and determination and courage to force it down the throats of those who will resist.

Our steps must be sure and bold and decisive because change is something that our country direly needs.

After all said and done, when we have turned a new page, all of us, every Nigerian, will be swept to a new place where we would find our collective soul regurgitated from the bowels of the monstrous beast called corruption.

CHAPTER FIVE

IMPEDIMENTS TO REFORMS IN NIGERIA

There is a rational against all things but none is worse than the
rational against positive change

THE PRIMAL IMPEDIMENT TO THE kinds of reforms Nigeria needs in order to make it work for every Nigerian is Nigerians.

It is not that Nigerians do not know how to make their country work; it is just that they are not interested in making it work.

It reflects in our refusal to acknowledge the fact that something drastic and urgent needs to be done to preserve our country.

It reflects in our refusal to do the heavy lifting required to hoist our country on a pedestal of sustainability.

It reflects in our reticence about imbibing principles and concepts that will guarantee that Nigeria rejuvenates as a dynamic and progressive country.

It is not that Nigerians cannot, it is just that Nigerians will not. And that is the real crux of the matter.

Even when Nigerians try to do something, it is only on a whim and they do so half-heartedly and with heavy-footed hesitation.

The sad reality that Nigerians will not lift a finger to reform their country in any meaningful way mainly stems from the fact that Nigerians have no sense of country.

It is also possible that most Nigerians have not had the disposition to fully embrace the various reform agenda that have so far been tried out by various regimes because they lacked confidence in the reform ideas.

Perhaps, a more inclusive, more comprehensive, more realistic, more sensible reform agenda will serve to inspire and infuse the much needed confidence and produce the kind of engagement and participation that would yield the much needed reform dividends.

Another major obstacle to meaningful and sustainable reforms in Nigeria is the prevailing mindset amongst Nigerians and non-Nigerians alike that meaningful reform is impossible in Nigeria either because the country is beyond salvation or because Nigerians are inherently incapable of reforming their country.

Unfortunately, it is this sense of resignation and indifference that has made it possible for the rot in Nigeria to perpetuate.

Because people are nonchalant about the goings-on around them, those who foment the malaises that plague Nigeria do so without inhibitions.

This attitude is usually marked by a shrug of the shoulders and a flippant non-committal *"e-no concern me, e no be my papa business"* which suggests that as long as one is not personally affected, one should not be bothered by the decay and madness all around.

Then there is the misguided belief in some quarters that a

Nigeria that is efficient and is founded on principles of fairness and equity will not augur well for certain ethnic groups.

Indeed, there are those who wrongly believe that if things were done properly in Nigeria they would receive less than what they are currently receiving.

And there are those who believe that their best chance of reaping significant benefits from the oil resources of Nigeria is to have a lopsided, inefficient, and perverse system that surreptitiously disadvantages one part of Nigeria and benefits another. Or a system that bends over backwards to overcompensate a part of Nigeria on the mere assumption that because it does not produce wealth, it is disadvantaged.

For example, there are people in Northern Nigeria who assume that the best way for the North to continue to benefit from the vast oil resources of the South is to maintain control of the national power machinery even if it means doing so by preserving the dysfunctional status quo and sustaining perverse and inequitable structures.

However, it is possible to have a fair and balanced system that ensures that no ethnic group is given a short shrift in the scheme of things.

It is possible to have a system that guarantees that every ethnic group in Nigeria has equal stakes while at the same time ensuring that those who have been directly impacted by resource production receive just compensation.

Perhaps, the most detrimental mindset that threatens potential reforms in Nigeria is the belief by almost every Nigerian one comes across that God has a hand in or can influence political and situational outcomes in Nigeria.

Nigerians have become hyper-religious in the last two decades to the extent that most actually believe that God would intervene on their behalf to set their country aright.

Indeed the pulse and heartbeat of religion in Nigeria have become so overwhelmingly pervasive that a person dropping in from Mars would think that Religion was born and bred in Nigeria and that God is actually a Nigerian citizen.

God is a major feature and theme of every conversation and every expectation and every personal and public activity to the extent that one cannot help but wonder why if indeed God is paramount in everything Nigerians do, how it is that the county is in so much disarray.

Listening in on the chatter in the course of the 2011 elections, it was both interesting and disheartening to see how much of the God angle was infused into the discourse about who should win elections and who should not; that some candidates were more God-fearing than others and deserved to be elected.

Unfortunately religion and religious differences became pivotal issues in the elections to the extent that some people even played the presidential elections as a tussle of religious faiths between the predominantly Christian south and the predominantly Muslim north.

The notion that God should be a factor in the election of Nigeria's political leadership and the belief that it is in God's place to reform Nigeria not only exposes the deep frustrations of most Nigerians about the state of affairs in their country, but a shows a remarkable hopelessness that their country can be reformed by the acts of human beings.

The expectation that God should drive the engine of reforms in Nigeria is a sad reflection of how much Nigerians' sense of reality has been eroded and replaced with sheer fantasy and wishful thinking. It is a totally misguided and misplaced mindset that heavily underscores the difficulty that any reform agenda that is not faith-based will encounter.

However, there is a possibility that when actual and working reforms are instituted and Nigeria begins to turn a new leaf, God would step away from the limelight of public engagement and recede back into the confines of personal lives.

The other major obstacles to reforms in Nigeria can be summed up in three categories.

First is the mindset that Nigerians have to be reformed first before their country can be reformed; that the system will be efficient only when the people who operate it have imbibed the virtues of efficiency; that people cannot comport to good behavior unless they are purged of bad behavior.

Second is the mediocre notion that Nigeria's democracy needs time to grow and mature before Nigerians can experience a viable democracy; that the kinds of decent and efficient democracies practiced in places like the United States, France and Canada just to name a few, are unobtainable in Nigeria because Nigeria's democracy is still in its infancy.

Third is that Nigerians rely too much on the supreme authority figure; that a person in a position of authority has absolute authority; that one person can have unbridled power and use it as he sees fit. Entrenched within this ridiculous premise is the assumption that Nigeria's best hope for salvation lies in the emergence of a responsible leadership; the expectation that one person can singularly set Nigeria on a right course.

Indeed most Nigerians have become incurable skeptics and ardent cynics about the possibility of salvation for their country.

Many have given up hope that no matter how hard one tries, one can never bring about any meaningful change in Nigeria.

And in order to buttress that standpoint, they have adduced and imbibed notions that derogate the possibility of sweeping reforms in Nigeria.

To begin with, the notion that Nigerians are incapable of reforming their country because they are inherently bad and undisciplined is absolute nonsense.

It is common to hear people assert that Nigeria is not working for majority of Nigerians because Nigerians are uncouth or uncivilized or predisposed to bad behavior.

For this reason, most people wrongly believe that the only way to reform Nigeria is to first and foremost reform the people or readjust their moral and political compasses.

This simple-minded notion is completely misplaced if not ignorant.

Nigerians are not bad or corrupt because they are Nigerians; they are bad or corrupt because they are human beings, period.

Every human being has an inherent nature to be bad and conscienceless. That is why political systems and efficient social and economic structures were developed to help keep people in check.

The typical Nigerian is not worse than the typical American and the typical Nigerian is not much different from the typical American or Canadian or French or English.

The difference between the Nigerian and the American is that one, the American is compelled to comport to good behavior by the efficient and curtailing socio-political and technological structures that are in place in America and the other, the Nigerian is compelled to comport to bad behavior by the absence of efficient and curtailing socio-political and technological structures in Nigeria.

It is not because the average American is created with special qualities or equipped with special attributes that makes him more responsible to his community and more mindful of his civic responsibilities than the average Nigerian, it is because the American has mechanisms of behavioral control within his community while the Nigerian has little or no inhibitions about how to conduct himself within an organized society.

Americans do not generally obey the laws of their country because they are generally morally upright people; they obey the laws of their country because they have an efficient system of enforcing their laws. Conversely, Nigerians do not obey the laws of their country because there is no efficient system of enforcing the laws of their country.

In America if you are caught speeding beyond the posted limit you will get a ticket and if you drink and drive you will pay dearly. The American policeman is well trained and well equipped to catch you and if he takes you before a judge, you may even go to jail.

In Nigeria there are no posted speed limits much less any requirement that you keep to certain limits for that matter. There is no one to hold you accountable if you drink and drive. You drive as fast as the road permits. The only thing to limit your speed is bad roads. The policeman on the corner is only on the corner to extort money from you.

Americans are generally not corrupt because they have an efficient system of checks and balances that hold them accountable for their actions and answerable for their shortcomings. Conversely, Nigerians are generally corrupt because there is no efficient system of checks and balances and people are not held accountable and answerable for their misdeeds.

Indeed one of the most endearing facets of American society is that it thrives on an inbuilt adversarial device which affords every citizen the incentive to be the watchdog of society.

In America, there is a reward incentive for doing something good that benefits the general public positively. A heroic act of saving a stranger's life or exposing untoward deeds by your neighbor would certainly fetch you fifteen minutes of fame on national television and possibly a book deal to boot.

This encourages people to look to the next person as a possible meal ticket or an opportunity to prime time exposure and keeps everyone on tiptoes.

The internalized mechanism of checks and balances also assures that people are mindful of who is paying attention to their actions and discourages them from conducts that are detrimental to society.

In America, an individual cannot be the sole decision maker about how public money is spent and if a public official is caught stealing from government or public coffers he would be sent to jail.

In Nigeria, one person can be the sole decision maker about how public money is spent and if he is caught stealing from public coffers he would be celebrated and hailed as a *"sharp"* or *"smart"* man.

Americans generally have a say in how their country is governed because they have an efficient electoral system that ensures that they can rely on the power of their vote and guarantees that every vote counts.

Conversely, Nigerians have no say in how their country is

governed because they do not have an efficient electoral system that guarantees anything.

In America, the politician campaigns hard on principles and ideologies and hopes that people will buy his ideas for governance and give him their vote.

In Nigeria, the politician has no political ideology and is only interested in how to outsmart his opponents in rigging the vote.

Americans know that if they commit a crime, it is only a matter of time before they are caught and punished because they have an effective law enforcement system and an efficient judiciary that works to protect people.

Nigerians know they can commit a crime and get away with it because they do not have a system of law enforcement that is effective and a judicial system that works to protect people.

In America, no matter how highly placed and highly connected and wealthy the criminal is, he will be brought to justice and he will pay dearly for his crime.

In Nigeria, the criminal will be let off the hook as soon as he can grease the palms of law enforcement personnel and the judge with hefty sums of money and if he is highly placed and highly connected, he would not even be in the hook in the first place.

The bottom line therefore, is that it is the system that makes people either good or bad. If the system is efficient, people are compelled to be good and if it is inefficient, people are encouraged to be bad.

To say that Nigerians must first be like Americans before they can build and develop their country is hokum. And the suggestion that the Nigerian politician must first eschew the virtues of honesty and commitment to service before Nigeria's political terrain can be viable is without merit.

The point to be taken here is neither that the systems in place in America are 100% efficient nor that America does not have problems, the point is that America's systems are far more efficient than Nigeria's and that explains why one works for its citizens and the other does not.

If more efficient systems and structures are instituted in Nigeria, Nigerians would generally behave well. If they are compelled to be disciplined and responsible, Nigerians will be disciplined and responsible.

A typical example of this possibility is the monthly sanitation exercise instituted by Generals Buhari and Idiagbon when they came to power in 1983. On the first Saturday of every month, activities and movement of people were restricted for a few hours during which Nigerians were required to clean up their neighborhoods. This worked out quite well for a while because it was strictly enforced with a few exemptions.

Although there are well-intentioned laws and regulations in Nigeria, most of these laws and regulations are not supported by structures that make implementing or enforcing them possible.

For examples, you cannot require and expect people not to dump refuse in the streets when you have not provided them with an efficient system of refuse disposal. And you cannot require and expect people to pay their electricity bills when you have not provided an efficient system of supply and billing.

In the final analysis, it is the system that should drive the behavior of people and not the other way round.

People should not be expected to comport to law and order if the methods of enforcing the law are in shambles or nonexistent. The most reasonable thing to expect is that if the system is reformed, the people will have no choice than to conform.

Therefore, for meaningful and sustainable reforms to be instituted in Nigeria, focus must center on structures and not on people.

Then there is the scatterbrain notion that Nigeria's democracy needs time to grow and mature.

This is completely baseless, out of whack and unfortunately, permeates the consciousness of most Nigerians.

This simplistic excuse for Nigeria's pathetic democracy ten years after it was instituted is based on old worn out clichés such as, "*Rome was not built in a day*" and "*practice makes perfect*".

If Rome was not built in a day, is it not possible that the idea of what Rome would look like after it is built may have been forged in a day?

Also, is it not the case that practice can only make perfect if the practice is in the right direction and if it is founded on a sound and firm footing?

If practice is in the wrong direction and founded on unsound and unsteady footing, then things can only take a turn for the worse and not for the better.

You cannot expect good outcomes when you are trotting down a path that will produce bad outcomes.

This explains exactly why, ten years after, Nigeria's democracy rather than improving, continues to falter.

It explains why Nigerians have been making the same mistakes over and over without making any significant progress.

"It took America more than two hundred years to get to where America is today." One Nigerian politician once quipped in defense of the pitiable political clime in Nigeria. "We are just starting," he concluded.

"Just starting? Ten years and you are just starting?" I could not resist retorting.

However, in making that assertion, the politician exposed his total ignorance of the fact that although the democratic principles that shape America were conceived more than two hundred years ago, America's founding fathers had the foresight and visionary brilliance to institute a process that would stand the test of time.

The notion that Nigeria is a young democracy and therefore needs time to grow is hinged on the assumption that with years of practice, Nigerians will become better at managing their democracy.

It is akin to saying that for us to be technologically savvy in the 21st century we need to start from basic or primitive technological concepts rather than the advanced technological ideas of today.

It is also analogous to saying that in order for us to become good at making cars; we have to start by making tricycles and in order for us to have a reliable and computerized system of balloting, we have to start by the crude method of requiring people to signify their voting intent by raising their hands.

The notion is also a lame excuse for the inability or failure of Nigerians to fashion a model democracy that works for every Nigerian from the get-go.

We had the opportunity of instituting a vibrant 21st century democracy that is tailored to the Nigerian socio-cultural clime when we restarted our democratic process in 1999 but we did not utilize that opportunity. Rather we decided to institute a mediocre process and hoped that the more we practiced it the better it would become.

Sadly, the people who make these lame excuses and who think we need to start from the basic and improve to the advanced are the very same people who would buy the latest technologies in cars and electronics for themselves rather than start out with mediocre automobiles and improve one day to the advanced.

The same Nigerians who have become adept at copying just about anything from the latest ideas in music and entertainment and fashion are the same people who would prefer we settle for basic and mediocre forms of politics, infrastructure and economy.

For their personal purposes, they want the best, the most advanced, the most efficient and the most up-to-date; for their country they want the least functional and least efficient and the least advanced. How sad.

When it is for themselves it has to be classy and they would go to any length to get what they want but when it is for their country, it can only be crass and there is no desire to do better.

When it is for themselves, they justify their state-of-the-art choices with the most ridiculous and most outrageous arguments such as "they deserve the best" but when it is for their country they would excuse it with the lamest and most obnoxious reasoning such as "we have to start from somewhere".

These people have to be made to understand that if we wanted an experimental democratic process in Nigeria, we would have elected experimental politicians and given them experimental powers.

There is no excuse and no rational for why Nigerians cannot have a 21st century democracy in a 21st century Nigeria.

We cannot take time to grow our democracy; we can institute a mature democracy that is tailored to our needs and one that works for all Nigerians in the 21st century today.

Similarly, there is no excuse why Nigeria cannot have

infrastructure and amenities comparable to those in countries in Europe, Asia and America.

General Gowon who was military leader from 1966 to 1975 demonstrated that if a handsome chunk of the proceeds from our oil resources was directed to infrastructure development, Nigeria would have far better road networks, uninterrupted electricity supply, ceaselessly flowing portable water and other basic amenities than many of the so-called developed countries.

Imagine what Nigeria would be like today if we had followed that precedent and invested in maintaining and modernizing Nigeria's infrastructure rather than stuffing private coffers and amassing personal wealth.

Imagine how dynamic Nigeria's economy would be today if we had good infrastructure and security. Imagine what the living standards of majority of Nigerians would be today if we had invested in our country rather than losing the money to a handful of Nigerians.

Unfortunately, in the last few decades, Nigeria has very little to show infrastructure-wise for the billions of dollars it has wracked up in earnings from oil. The only structures that have kept up with the times are personal mansions and private comforts.

It is therefore imperative for any sustainable reform to get off the mindset that we have to start mediocre and grow to be better.

Nigeria can have the best in everything right now if Nigerians mean it.

Finally, Nigerians rely too heavily on the notion of a messianic leadership, a leadership which should at a time of its own choosing right the wrongs of society but is not necessarily obligated to do so.

Recall the recent chatter about the 2011 elections. It sounded like Nigerians were about to choose a messiah or a benevolent dictator with the powers to do and undo.

Nigerians have unbridled and sometimes blind, unquestioning faith and unnecessary respect for authority and leadership.

This is one sad legacy of the decades of military leadership to which Nigerians were subjected for a good part of the country's fifty years history.

Because they have become accustomed to the ways of military dictatorship, Nigerians will not challenge or question authority.

They believe that he who has authority cannot be wrong. And in charting an epileptic political course, this notion has been imbibed and carried forth by the emergent democratic leadership which has carried their political office as if they were a military dictatorship.

In addition to the military psyche, the Nigerian, no matter what ethnicity he comes from, is accustomed to the notion of the all-powerful authority figure and is readily agreeable and amenable to absolute authority.

The three principal ethnic components, Hausa-Fulani, Yoruba, and Igbo, and their subcomponents as well had and have cultural and traditional value systems that revolved and still revolves around unalloyed and undiluted respect and glorification of wealth and position.

This explains why Nigerians expect the president to single-handedly dictate the course of things in Nigeria and to have the power to simply decide and implement a policy at will and as he sees fit.

For examples, many believe the president has the powers to provide electricity or to build roads without consulting anyone.

Indeed this belief is borne out by the fact that that is exactly the case in practice. It is true that the political official in Nigeria has immense powers and although an anomaly, it is acceptable by most Nigerians.

Because of this also, Nigerians do not perceive or see leadership as position of service rather they see and perceive leadership as position of supreme authority.

They see appointment of a person to a public office as a personal elevation for a personal opportunity and will scoff at a person who returns from public office without personal wealth to show for his time in office.

"*Ah, the man own don better! God don butter his bread!*" I'm sure you have heard this popular quip before about someone receiving a new appointment.

Also the person who has authority has power beyond reproach and can flaunt and brandish it with impunity.

Recall the last time you encountered a Nigerian with any level of official authority or position of importance whether in Nigeria or abroad. Recall his or her attitude towards you and the way he or she brandished his or her authority as if he or she was some god.

Some guy you used to know and hang out with around the neighborhood receives an appointment to some office and all of a sudden he is no longer reachable. He begins to carry himself with his shoulders puffed up as if he now owns the world. He goes through an attitudinal transformation and believes that now that his circumstance has changed, he has "*arrived*" and deserves to be worshipped.

As it is, too much authority resides at the hands of one person in Nigeria and this is bad for the country because as we all know, *power corrupts and absolute power corrupts absolutely.*

In Nigeria's case, power intoxicates and absolute power confers a status of deity.

Consider the recent pronouncement by the chairman of the Independent Electoral Commission (INEC) prior to the 2011 elections that he would not hesitate to nullify any election that he, INEC chairman, determines to be flawed.

This is a typical example of power deifying a person upon whom it is conferred and says a lot about the state of affairs in Nigeria.

The INEC chairman's chest-thudding declaration presupposes that he has the singular authority to determine the outcome of an election; that he could, singularly, without due process and hearing, determine that an election was not properly conducted and nullify it.

Consider also this situation where a policeman at a road block threatened to arrest me and lock me up at his station for asking him why he was demanding that I produce the bill-of-lading for my car.

The fact that he could actually do what he was threatening to do and get away with it makes the reality about exercise of power and abuse of power in Nigeria all the more frightening.

Flowing from the notion of unbridled authority are other similar assumptions; the big man with a fat wallet, the all-important, society fat cat with gushing questionable wealth, must know it all and what he says must not be questioned.

The person that has wealth has wisdom and is in position to tell others what to do.

The little, inconsequential man has no knowledge and must not have anything to contribute.

The expectation that one person in authority can single-handedly transform a nation may be appropriate in military style dictatorship but not in a democracy which demands collective action.

For meaningful and sustainable reforms to be instituted in Nigeria, Nigerians have to be weaned from these false notions and made to realize that it is not up to one person of authority to decide what is good or what is not good for the country.

Nigerians must discountenance the expectation that a single person with authority should have the ability to transform the nation and come to terms with the reality that a democracy can also be conducted like a dictatorship which is exactly what we have in Nigeria today.

Most importantly, Nigerians must realize that change cannot come from their leadership and must make up their minds whether they want a democracy or a dictatorship.

Chapter Six

ROADMAP TO REFORMS IN NIGERIA

It is not less difficult when there is a will but it is certainly easier when there is a way

Nothing short of a clean sweep would bring about the kind of country that majority of Nigerians deserve.

Because every sector and aspect of Nigeria is in decay and every sector and aspect is interconnected, we have to start from scratch to redefine and restructure the country in order for it to work.

We cannot afford to "start from somewhere" or "take one step at a time" as most people and certainly the present political leadership in Nigeria would prefer.

To reform Nigeria, we must think in terms of wide-ranging, leave-nothing-to-chance, all-inclusive, no-holds-barred, comprehensive reforms that would touch on every aspect and every pore of the country.

Nigeria is like the fingers of a hand; all the fingers are sullied with stench and rot. If we clean one finger and leave the rest unclean, it is only a matter of time before the lone clean finger will be sullied again and if we clean four and leave one unclean, same thing would happen.

Nigeria is like a garbage-filled five-room house. We cannot clean one room and expect that it would stay clean. If we do not have a plan of cleaning the entire house at once, it is only a matter of time before the garbage spills over into the lone clean room.

For examples, we cannot curb corruption in governance without curbing corruption in the electoral system because if an electoral system is corrupt, it can only produce corrupt elected officials.

We cannot curb corruption in the way public contracts are executed without curbing corruption in the way they are awarded.

We cannot demand that a person be not corrupt and then leave him alone with the keys to our money vault.

To secure a house from thieves we must ensure that the entire perimeter of the house is break-in proof. No matter how much we reinforce the lock on the doors, the house remains vulnerable if we do nothing to reinforce the windows as well as other parts of the house.

In the same vein, we cannot assume that over time our system would clean itself up and we cannot wait for change to come to us; we have to seek and proactively pursue and capture change.

Also, we cannot depend on people who benefit from a rotten system to bring about meaningful and beneficial change because a pig cannot be expected of its own accord to clean its putrescent sty from which it derives great pleasure.

So far, efforts at cracking down on Nigeria's problems have been piecemeal and halfhearted and epileptic.

Consider the piecemeal, half-measure and lackadaisical type of action the Nigerian legislature took in 2010 by purportedly amending the 1999 constitution.

Rather than embarking on a clean sweep of a constitution that everyone agrees is seriously flawed in many respects, they decided to smooth out the rough edges on only portions that would make their ascent to power less cumbersome.

Also rather than embarking on a total, one-fell-swoop effort at reforming the electoral system in Nigeria, the Nigerian legislature expects that giving financial autonomy to the national election commission is the only ingredient needed to make it truly independent.

We have tried such knee-jerk, reactionary, tepid and sporadic approaches to reforms before and they have neither worked nor produced sustainable results. Each effort has been marked by false-starts and unpropitious outcomes.

We have had a revolving door of reactionary prosecutions and incarceration of countless corrupt public officials and politicians as a way of curbing corruption since the days General Murtala Mohammed took office in 1975 but they have not yielded sustainable results.

General Murtala Mohammed who came to power on the back of a military coup was courageous and incensed against corruption. He had the right attitude but the wrong ideas about tackling the scourge.

Corruption was the primal reason why Mohammed overthrew the government of General Gowon. However, while Mohammed dealt a formidable blow against corruption at the civil service level, he allowed many corrupt people to hang around his military administration. He would pay dearly with his life barely months after he took office and dared to challenge the status quo.

Mohammed failed because he believed that the problem of corruption was limited to the Nigerian civil service. He failed to see that it permeated every camber and crevice of Nigeria.

While he busied himself with trying to clean the muck in the civil service, he was unaware of the cold-blooded conspiracy in the top military ranks to hack him down.

General Obasanjo came to power in 1976 after Mohammed was slain in a partially successful coup, holding himself out as tooled in the spirit and temper of Murtala Mohammed but not quite his zeal. And it was understandable why he took a mellower path than his predecessor.

Although he railed against official graft, Obasanjo consciously shied away from taking the kind of bold risks that cost Mohammed his life. In the end, he was more of a pacifist against corruption than a reformer and purist.

Shehu Shagari became first civilian President in 1979 at the inception of Nigeria's second attempt at democracy and because he was a former school teacher and an "*honest man*" when he was a minister in the first Republic, Nigerians assumed that Shagari was the man to infuse decorum and sanity in the system.

Ironically as at 1979, most Nigerians were sure that corruption was purely a military thing and most Nigerians were convinced that a civilian democracy automatically would translate to good and uncorrupt governance.

Incidentally, this was also the misguided prevalent belief in 1999 when the current democracy was instituted after decades of military rule of the country.

Shagari himself would bah-bah against graft and corruption

and even went as far as instituting an anti-corruption commission that ultimately went nowhere.

Under Shagari's administration, corruption took on a whole new meaning; it actually became a way of life in Nigeria and provided a perfect excuse for a bunch of incensed military brass to rend the civilian administration five years later.

Generals Buhari and Idiagbon came to power in 1983 brandishing a blazing *Damoclean* sword of retribution and indictment against widespread corruption and indiscipline in Nigeria.

They adopted the Mohammed-style template of hounding, dismissal and imprisonment of corrupt people and deigned to clean up the rot in Nigeria.

However, they too failed to follow the unwritten rules on how not to attempt to clean the Augean Stables that is Nigeria which Murtala Mohammed had unwittingly made by his own ill-fated attempt.

Buhari and Idiagbon had the heart and the motivation, but they lacked the kind of vision and brutal enterprise that folks like Colonel Rawlings had displayed in Ghana.

They did not quite think their strategies through and realized when it was too late that corruption in Nigeria was like a hydra-headed monster. You cannot kill it by cutting off a few heads. You can only kill it by cutting off every one of its monstrous heads.

General Babangida came to power in 1985 by sacking Generals Buhari and Idiagbon from power in what was touted as a palace coup.

Babangida's excuse for handing Buhari and Idiagbon their pink slips was that Buhari and Idiagbon were too heavy-handed and too brutal in their exercise of power and were not properly dealing with the problem of corruption and indiscipline.

Well, can anyone imagine Babangida of all people trying to solve the problem of corruption in Nigeria? Well, he too did try in his own way to curb corruption.

Although Babangida dealt some flaccid blows to wayward bankers and confiscated properties of corrupt civil servants during his regime, he turned out to be a master at perpetrating corruption and an "evil genius" at manipulation.

In 1993 Ernest Shonekan a bark-less, toothless puppy was appointed to head an epileptic transitional government after Babangida annulled the presidential elections results of the same year.

There was not much Shonekan could do by way of governance, so he groped around like a man who had lost his way in the dark until he was thrown out by a ferocious General Sani Abacha barely three months after.

Even Abacha was animatedly ferocious against corruption and aggressively persecuted only those he felt were corrupt in his own eyes and in his own estimation. However, Abacha was corruption personified and he effectively used it as a tool for manipulation and control.

General Abubakar who took the center stage after Abacha suddenly died in 1998 did not lift a finger to address the myriad of problems in Nigeria.

Abubakar appeared to care for only one thing; to allow as much looting as possible and get out of the way. And he did just that. And before anyone could say "oh no, not again", Obasanjo was back in power as a democratically elected president.

Obasanjo retook the center stage with his rail-much-do-little attitude towards corruption in Nigeria in 1999. He was visibly livid with temper-tantrums against corruption but behind the scenes, he quietly embraced it for his own purposes.

In public, he bared his fangs by instituting and empowering the Economic and Financial Crimes Commission, EFCC and it became a vicious force to hound and harass his political foes and people Obasanjo did not just like.

Like his predecessor, Yar'Adua became a champion crusader against corruption and was vociferous in favor of reforms when he ascended the political throne in 2008 and sought to expand on the efforts of Obasanjo with very little impact and sustainable results.

Goodluck Jonathan who took over the reins of power when Yar'Adua kicked the bucket in 2010 has merely continued in the old ways and appears to be reluctant to take bold actions even with his election to a fresh term of office.

The foregoing historical snapshots of the attempts to battle the scourge of corruption in Nigeria underscore the fact that we have not at any given time and opportunity really sat down to think hard enough about what is effective and what is not; what will work and what will not.

Unfortunately, we have tended to use the same methods over and over again and have not realized that they have not worked and will never work.

Just like so many other efforts to date to advance Nigeria politically and economically such as Obasanjo's Operation Feed the Nation (OFN) in 1976 and Shagari's Green Revolution in 1979, we have tended to do things in a way that broaches and bestrides rather than effectively tackles and solves the problem.

The idea of relying on deterrence by prosecution and punishment after the fact has not and will not work to battle the scourge of corruption in Nigeria.

The corrupt Nigerian is not thinking repercussion when he is stealing public funds; he is thinking and believing he can get away with it.

There is an incentive for corruption in Nigeria because there are numerous examples of people who stole from public coffers and got away with it. Chances are 99 in 100 that anyone who steals today will go scot-free.

Emphasis on the battle against corruption must therefore rest on installing preventive structural and systemic mechanisms that would make it difficult for people to be corrupt and then backing it up with sincere and fair-minded arrest and prosecution based on a fair process of rule of law. Prevention should be primary; prosecution should be secondary.

As we have seen, fear of prosecution alone is simply not enough. Rather than waiting to make a person pay for being corrupt, the proper attitude is to make it impossible for anyone to be corrupt. And if a person manages to slip through the cracks, the full wrath of the law would be brought upon him.

As we have seen from the historical snapshots above and from the current goings-on in Nigeria, Nigerians cannot rely on their leaders to reform Nigeria because their efforts have been mostly half measures.

We cannot wait for a messianic leader to lift the country out of the misery of our collective corrupt state of mind. It is now the duty of every Nigerian.

Unfortunately, Nigeria can no longer afford experiments and trials and errors that have characterized our efforts at reforms so far.

It is now time to take bold and decisive action. It is now time to take the bull by the horn and do the things that will actually make our country work.

And there are many practical and realistic ways to pursue and implement the kinds of reforms Nigeria needs.

The roadmap to reforms in the new dispensation is to get every Nigerian involved.

We must henceforth treat the pronouncements and actions of our political leadership with a dash of suspicion and question their so-called reform antics with three rudimentary questions: What would that do? What else needs be done? And why can't we do it now?

We must all be our own collective watchdogs and take on the patriotic responsibility of making sure that the man or woman standing next to us does not get away with the bounty he or she has looted from our national coffers.

The average Nigerian understands that the millions of naira and dollars stolen from the national coffers yearly by a few people belong to all Nigerians.

The average Nigerian is witness to the thievery all around him or her but the average Nigerian still looks on with indifference and complacence.

Nigerians are complacent to corruption because no one has projected to them a sensible and realistic method of resistance and activism and change.

The starting point of the push for reform would therefore be to re-instill in the Nigerian the will to resist.

Most Nigerians are skeptical of activism for reforms because the messaging by activists have been non-committal and discordant and lacked a clear sense of what needs to be done.

However, most Nigerians will become a part of a movement for reforms with realistic and realizable goals. And that is the spirit that any effort at reforms must tap into.

One outstanding feature of past attempts at reforms is the zeal and hopefulness with which Nigerians embraced those efforts. The failures of those efforts were therefore not as a result of lack of support from Nigerians, they failed because they were not properly articulated, designed and implemented to ensure success and sustainability.

One veritable path to resisting corruption would be to make life a little bit uncomfortable and untenable for those who have chosen the path of corruption.

Nigerians have to be made aware that the big car that the big politician is driving after having stolen from public coffers is not his car. It is the people's car and any Nigerian is free to take a ride in that car.

The big house that the politician has built is the peoples' house and any Nigerian is free to go in there for shelter and for food.

Unless the politician can demonstrate by clear and convincing evidence that the wealth he has amassed was out of personal sweat, the wealth belongs to all.

We know the politician very well. We have known him all his life. We knew when he was born, when he went to school, what he did afterwards, and we know there is no way he could have amassed the kind of money with which he is building the mansion in his village.

We know that he only started doing "very well" when he got into political office. There is no way his salary as a public servant could get him the kind of mansion he is building next door. He could only have stolen the money or he got it through corrupt means. The house, when it is all built, is community property and the people are free to go in there for shelter or for meetings.

As soon as the mansion starts going up, people should rally together and demand that the politician explains the source of the funds with which he is building the house. As soon as he pulls up with the big car we know he cannot afford, we should step up to him and ask him to explain.

However, this is only a step to force the hands of our political leaders to eschew bad behavior and institute the reforms the country direly needs.

True and lasting reform can only be achieved when we have erected mechanisms and systems that make it more difficult if not impossible for corruption to occur because like everyone knows, "prevention is better than cure".

Before there was corruption and decay and ineptitude and conscienceless public office holders, there were decent, forthright, service-oriented, and conscientious people.

Before Nigeria embraced filth and rancor and decadence there was decency and mutual respect and moderateness.

Although most Nigerians have written off their country and have concluded that Nigeria cannot be reformed, there is a way out because before there was mass scale corruption, there was a fairly decent Nigeria.

Although most Nigerians are ambivalent and non-committal to the prospects and possibilities of reforms in Nigeria, there is hope for a new day because just like they did when they held out hope for past efforts at reform, most Nigerians are willing to embrace meaningful and sensible change.

If we sweep our country clean and install an efficient mechanism for keeping dirt out, the country will stay clean. Institute an effective system of security and checks and balances and the thieving politician will be discouraged when he returns.

This is the duty Nigerians owe their country.

PART II

SOLVING NIGERIA'S PROBLEMS

CHAPTER SEVEN

BRAND NEW CONSTITUTION FOR A BRAND NEW NIGERIA

Our organizing principles should not bewilder and confound us but enlighten and preserve us

THE FIRST THING WE MUST do to reform and renew Nigeria so that it truly works for every Nigerian is to discard our present constitution, including the recent much-touted cosmetic amendments, and begin from scratch to create a new set of organizing principles that makes sense, is suited for Nigeria, and is understandable by the average Nigerian.

The new constitution must be one that gives cognizance to the aspirations and hopes of every Nigerian irrespective of creed, status or tribe.

The new constitution must empower every Nigerian irrespective of his or her ethnic or religious proclivity and afford him or her unfettered opportunity to pursue his or her life's goals within his or her community.

Above all else, the new constitution must no longer impliedly define Nigeria as a country of competing ethnicities rather it must categorically assert that Nigeria is a country of individuals, each with his or her own individual and distinct character and purpose that is not tied to ethnic affinity.

The primal goal of the new constitution must be to protect and preserve the rights, privileges and freedoms of each and every citizen of Nigeria without equivocation and guarantee that the fundamental rights conferred upon him or her by natural assignment are inalienable.

The 1999 Nigerian constitution under which Nigeria's present democracy operates is actually a regurgitated and barely refurbished version of previous constitutions that were produced under the auspices of military regimes.

This is not to say that the constitution is bad merely because it was a handiwork of the military as many in Nigeria presume, it is only bad because it is on its face a poorly articulated document.

The 1999 constitution was cobbled together by the military regime of General Abubakar in 1998 with the purported participation of political stalwarts from around Nigeria.

In other words, when General Abubakar summoned a constitutional conference in 1998, it was actually a charade, an unproductive money guzzling binge that was never intended to put Nigeria in a better stead.

What Abubakar succeeded in doing was to invite a cadre of self-appointed political hogs to sit around in Abuja and do nothing more than dusting up the old book and proclaiming it new because it is hard to imagine that the shallow and ridiculous document which Nigeria parades as its constitution was put together by sensible and competent people.

Although it presumes to embrace core principles of democracy premised on the American model, the 1999 constitution is a patchwork of many convoluted and redundant ideas.

It is a sham and laughable document riddled with redundant chapters, inconsistent clauses, overarching sections and contradictory subsections that makes understanding it a painful, pitiful and ridiculous exercise and upholding it a fruitless and fortuitous venture.

It is very possible that not many of the people who parade themselves as politicians and government officials and leaders and political experts and stalwarts have even looked at the document much less understanding it because if they did, perhaps things would been a little different in Nigeria today.

It is not surprising therefore that Nigeria is the way it is; a lawless, inept, ramshackle democracy where the powerful live by their own rules and the powerless are helpless and hopeless and are without any enforceable guarantees of protection in a country they call their own.

It is not at all surprising also that politics and governance in Nigeria is a laughable gimmick controlled by people who have no regard for constitutional order.

From every indication, it does appear that the Nigerian constitution was cobbled together as a mere formality and was never intended to have a clear meaning and to be taken seriously.

For instance, how does one reconcile the inconsistency between Section 3(1) of Chapter 1, Part I (General Provisions) which declaratorily forecloses the fact that there *shall* be 36 states in Nigeria with Section 8(1) of Chapter 1, Part II (Powers of the Federal Republic of Nigeria) which purports to give the National Assembly the power to create more states?

Does it mean that the constitution would first have to be amended to abrogate Section 3(1) before an additional state is created under Section 8(1)? Or will the state be created first before the change can be made? Unfortunately, the constitution is replete with many such conflicting ideas and notions.

From the way Nigerian politicians conduct themselves, it appears that the constitution was intentionally designed as a compilation of every imaginable dos and don'ts that were never intended to be binding on any one and were never intended to be the basis of governance in Nigeria.

Sadly, the constitution upon which Nigeria's best hope lies today is very similar to a religious book which contains many painstaking details of many interesting and boring items and events which are not particularly necessary to make a person a devout religious person.

It is similar to a religious book in the sense that as a religious devotee only goes to a specific verse to satisfy a specific purpose without giving consideration to what other verses have to say on the issue, so too does the Nigerian politician go to a specific section or subsection of the constitution to satisfy a specific political purpose without giving consideration to what other parts have to say on the issue.

The Nigerian constitution is also similar to a religious book in the sense that neither was ever meant to be understood or applied as a whole.

In other words, the constitution is merely, as Nigerians would say, "*for fancy*"; something we had to have just because it is fashionable for a country to have a document like that.

A read through the present Nigerian constitution will leave

anyone with a sound mind wondering what exactly the document is talking about and what it is intended to achieve.

It is a torment of a read and a voluminous extravagance of conflicting ideas, contradictory notions and endless rigmaroles.

It guarantees a specific right in one instance and abrogates it in another and gives a specific privilege in one instance and takes it away in another.

It is certain that a specific power belongs to the executive in one instance and in another, purports to give that same power to the legislature.

Recall the many disputes and heated debates regarding who is empowered to exercise certain authority between the federal legislature and the executive branch in the last ten years.

The constitution fails to succinctly delineate the powers of the three tiers; federal, states and LGAs and confuses the extent and character of their interaction and mutuality.

It mandates that political parties must reflect national character rather than allowing the political marketplace to determine the success of parties.

It presupposes that sovereignty belongs to the people of Nigeria from whom government through the Constitution derives all its powers and authority merely by declaring it rather than empowering it.

It browbeats that the security and welfare of the people is the primary purpose of government by merely stating it rather than asserting it in enforceable terms.

And it imagines that the participation by the people in their government is to be ensured in accordance with the provisions of the Constitution by merely asserting it rather than demanding it.

In short the Nigerian constitution is a massive joke. It smacks of a ridiculous and tedious document that was hurriedly put together by a bunch of over-enthusiastic, unthinking desperados who could not quite make up their minds about which of their many supposedly brilliant but confusing ideas to exclude from the document but finally settled for one which included every one of them.

The way the constitution is written somewhat suggests that the people who wrote it were not careful and deliberate and discerning and creative and painstaking, as if it was not really necessary to do so because the people for whom it was patched together were buffoons and nincompoops.

It looks like the folks at the constitutional conference randomly plucked ideas and concepts from different sources and lopped them together without careful thought about whether they made sense in the Nigerian context and without thorough consideration about whether they suited our clime.

In the end, what we have is a detailed, comprehensive and complex document that is so vast and rigorous in its enunciations and enumerations that it is painful to read and difficult to comprehend even for anyone with a university degree much less the uneducated man in the street.

It is not surprising therefore that most Nigerians do not even know what is in their constitution and what it portends for them mainly because it was not fashioned in a way that would make it accessible and understandable to every Nigerian.

It is a document that only highly discerning legal pundits and jurists can comprehend and even they too would be left scratching their heads trying to make sense out of it.

This is sad because in order to feel a sense of belonging and worth in his country, every Nigerian should be able to know what the organizing document of his country has in store for him.

The organizing document of any nation ought to set out in simple, plain and concise language the basic framework, structure and principles upon which the nation is organized and governed.

The constitution should be primarily an authority-giving and limiting instrument which establishes the basic parameters by which the authority it gives is to be exercised.

Surely we do not need four hundred pages, eight chapters, three hundred and twenty sections and a gazillion subsections for that.

The constitution ought not to be like a rule book or a comprehensive list of the laws of the land that specifies in details every dos and don'ts. It should merely delegate and assign powers and authority.

For instance, rather than containing a detailed recitation of how electoral commissions and officials are to be appointed and when and how elections would be conducted, it would have been enough for the Nigerian constitution to say that the president with the approval of the national assembly shall appoint an independent commission for the conduct of elections and such commission may fashion out rules and regulations for the free and fair conduct of elections as long as those rules and regulations do not abridge the right of the people to participate in the governance of their country.

As another example, rather than specifying the number of states and local governments or the number and character of executive bodies, it would have been sufficient for the constitution to say that the national legislature may, upon the petition of the people promulgate the creation or merger of states and local governments.

This would have removed the need of amending the constitution each time there is a need to increase or decrease the number of states or local governments or executive bodies.

The constitution of a nation should be the people's document and as a matter of technicality, the people should be presumed to have a say in what it looks like and what it contains.

This does not imply that every citizen of Nigeria must participate in or be consulted in order to draft a constitution that serves their needs. It does not also suggest that we must pool people from every region or nook and cranny of Nigeria together before we can have a constitution that is acceptable to all. We don't need a bunch of people to produce a document that would best reflect the aspirations of our dear country. In fact, one or two people would do.

Nigeria's constitution is principally the way it is because we have erroneously assumed that all parts of the country must be represented on the constitution drafting table before we can have a document that is truly Nigerian.

Any constitution that alienates the people by making it difficult for the people to understand what is contained in it does not deserve to be.

The present Nigerian constitution is an anomaly in that regard and should therefore be discarded and substituted with one that would make sense and be understandable to the average Nigerian.

Our constitution should neither sound foreign nor feel exotic to us and it should not just be a legal document with high sounding legalistic *isms*, disjointed *whereases*, perambulating *wherefores*, convoluting *notwithstandings* and annoying *foregoings*.

It should be a straightforward document which every Nigerian irrespective of educational attainment should be able to comprehend and appreciate.

What is most amazing about the Nigerian constitution is that many people in Nigeria agree that it is seriously flawed and yet nothing serious has been done to fix the problems.

Instead, Nigerian politicians and the leadership elite have only concerned themselves with aspects that benefit them and have failed to see that what the constitution needs is total overhaul and not piecemeal amendments.

What is also stupefying about Nigeria's constitutional imbroglio is the types of argument that have been put forward by people who think the piecemeal approach to fixing the numerous problems with the constitution is the best approach.

Some point to the constitution of the United States as an example of a constitution that was made better over many years by a continuous process of amendments.

Apart from incorrectly characterizing the American constitutional evolution, that type of argument ignores the reality that constitutional amendments are typically necessitated by arising needs and are used as an improvement mechanism rather than repair measure.

The 27 amendments to the US constitution were necessitated at various times by changes in the socio-political clime of the country and not because the original document was flawed. The original constitution adopted in 1787 was not flawed per se but was appropriate for the needs of the time.

Nigeria's constitution on the other hand is a flawed document from the get-go which did not sufficiently reflect the aspirations and temperaments of Nigeria as at the time it was adopted.

To rely on amendments as a way of repairing its many deficits would therefore require not only innumerable amendments but would take a very long time, the benefit of which we do not have, to make it right.

Nigeria does not have the luxury of another fifty years of tweaking in order to make its constitution right. We had the opportunity to get it right from the get-go and the fact that we did not should not make us embark on an endless repair process that would take forever to accomplish. The prudent thing to do is to start all over.

As a perspective, imagine what the US would do today if it had the benefit of coming up with a brand new constitution. No doubt, the document would be based on today's needs and not the needs of 1787.

In the same way, we did not have to begin from a crude constitution and work to repair it as an on-going process just because amendments sound romantic and are possible.

Unfortunately, this attitude reflects in many things Nigeria. Rather than seizing the opportunity to make things right the first time, we have imbibed the colonial mentality that we have to always start from somewhere mediocre as some people will readily say.

Constitutional amendments should not be an-ongoing process in Nigeria as many have suggested because it would have a destabilizing effect on the functioning of the country and create more uncertainty in the minds of Nigerians.

Nothing short of a total redo will repair the many shortcomings of Nigeria's present constitution. No amount of tinkering and burnishing and decoration will make good a house that is badly designed and erected on a ramshackle foundation.

For Nigeria to rejuvenate, the pitiable state of our constitution cannot be allowed to sustain. Without question, the sorry document that we call our constitution will have to be discarded if we hope to make our country work for all Nigerians.

The new Nigerian constitution must, aside from being concise and simple, be capable of being translated into the principal languages of our country so that its meanings and purposes are clearly understood and appreciated by all Nigerians.

CHAPTER EIGHT

CUT OUR CONSTITUTION ACCORDING TO OUR CLIME

Our organizing principles should be tailored to fit us and not us to fit them

ALTHOUGH TRUE FEDERALISM REMAINS NIGERIA'S best bet for sustainability, there is no doubt that the federal system mandated by the 1999 Nigerian constitution and which Nigeria purports to operate today is NOT one that is best suited for Nigeria.

A careful appraisal of the current Nigerian constitution and governance in Nigeria shows that Nigeria is far from practicing true federalism which raises even many more fundamental questions.

In fashioning and instituting our present constitution, did we take into consideration the peculiar and distinct nature and heritage as well as character of Nigeria to ensure that it effectively represents the aspirations and hopes of every Nigerian?

The answer is probably no because it appears that those who put the constitution together were primarily concerned about producing a document that is full of legalistic finesse and imaginative verbosity rather than one that is borne out of commonsense and practical simplicity.

Did we just copy our concept of federalism from somewhere just because it works somewhere else and ended up with a system that negates everything we hoped to achieve?

The answer is certainly yes because there is nothing original and exceptional about our mode of federalism.

Or did we need to look to other constitutional models to guide us in creating our own model and in the end created one that is antithetical to our well-being and progress?

The answer is a resounding yes because a mere look at the document shows a mélange of ideas that were hived from different constitutional models. There are ideas from all over; the French, the English, the Canadian, and the American.

Why could we not just sit down, tear a clean sheet from a writing pad and start from scratch without any existing model in mind?

We have had about nine good opportunities including five in the colonial era and four in the post-colonial era to try to come up with an organizing document for our country and all of the efforts have produced and regurgitated pretty much the same rickety and dysfunctional ideas.

Each time we have focused on restarting our democratic process we have tended to return again and again to the same old ideas that failed us in the past.

Rather than sitting down and hashing out new ideas, we have merely dusted up old ideas and made them new again with a few nondescript tweaks here and there. The only significant difference between the various constitutions is the dates on their blurbs.

Why did we even bother trying? And how many more times do we have to try before we get it right?

Perhaps the biggest failure of our constitution making process lies in the fact that we have failed to recognize the unique character and profile of our country.

We have equally failed to take into consideration that in terms of structure, ethnic temperament and cultural multiplicity, Nigeria is like no other country on earth and because of that we cannot simply borrow a system from somewhere else and expect that it would work for us.

Our constitution should be one that succinctly recognizes our character, correctly identifies our needs and effectively defines our collective purpose.

The federal system in place in Nigeria today is a sham Federalism. It is a federal system on paper while in practice, it is actually Unitarianism; a system that is suited perfectly for a military dictatorship which must out of necessity exert absolute control from the center.

The current Nigerian constitution to all intents and purposes has many practical shortcomings which cannot be adequately discussed here.

It touts a fictional autonomy for the states while in reality the states are entirely beholden and dependent on the federal government and to a large degree controlled by the federal government.

It harps on religious neutrality while in fact it tacitly ratifies and promotes the doctrine of one religion, Islam.

For instance, why should the constitution of Nigeria which is by-and-large a multi-religious, secular society authorize and endorse Islamic laws and Sharia courts?

Why should we have customary courts when we should be

operating a system of rule of law that is religion and culture neutral?

Why should customary courts be a trade-off for Sharia courts?

Why is it implied that Nigeria's laws come mainly from Judeo-Christian doctrines and should therefore be balanced with Muslim doctrines?

Why can't Nigeria's laws be strictly based on what works for humanity without trying to strike any unnecessary balances between competing religions?

As another example, the constitution touts the principles of separation of powers and checks and balances but in reality promotes concentration of powers in the hands of and to the benefit of the executive and creates an atmosphere for abuse and overextension of powers.

It is noteworthy to point out here that the federal system in place in Nigeria today was a creation of the military. It was specifically designed, shaped and instituted to comport with the hierarchical structures of the military and to serve military purposes.

What has happened is that in instituting our democracy, we have simply retained a military federal structure that is antithetical to the principles of civil democracy.

What we have been doing is trying to fit a square pole in a round hole and we have been foolish not to realize that what we have is a square pole and what is in front of us is a round hole.

In our ignorance and sheer stupidity, we have clothed ourselves in the most expensive apparel but we are wearing it the wrong side out.

We have donned the most expensive pair of shoes but we are

wearing the right shoe on the left foot and the left shoe on the right foot.

This is exactly why our democracy, no matter how long we practice it, will not yield any dividends.

Beginning with the presidency of Obasanjo and continuing until this day, we have seen a Judiciary and Legislature that are beholden to an all-powerful president. The president has the uncanny capacity to influence the outcome of a case before the highest court or to cajole a decision that favors his interests.

At the national center and across the 36 states, we have consistently seen an executive arm that acts more and more like a dictatorship.

Governors arm-twist legislators to pass laws that enlarge their personal purses and legislators kowtow to the wishes of governors and party machinery rather than to the welfare and well-being of the people.

Sadly also, the president controls everything and has been known to withhold his signature on contact papers for projects. His authority is rarely challenged by a Legislature whose members owe their election to the good graces of the president and party stalwarts.

The judiciary is a mere rubberstamp for the wishes of the president. And we are all back to the same old military-type exercise of authority.

It is no wonder then why each ethnic group would stake just about anything in other to secure control of the presidency or why politicians would go to any length to occupy an executive office in the country.

Although concentration of powers in the executive branch in practice presupposes that the problem is more of how people conduct governance rather than with the letter of the constitution, the constitution itself has created the problem by being very obtuse about the extent of the president's power and by giving too much power and influence to the president and executives across the states.

The first question we must ask and answer in forging a new constitutional path for Nigeria is whether federalism either in its truest and purest form or diluted and tempered form is even right for Nigeria in the first place.

In deciding on a constitutional path that is truly Nigerian in spirit and in essence, we must not merely pick up a list of forms of government in existence and then try to decide which best speaks to Nigeria's circumstance, we have to think in terms of which elements or subparts we can coral from whatever is out there and then refine and retune them to fit our clime.

And if at the end of the day it turns out that we have created an entirely new system of government that cannot easily be called by a particular name and cannot simply be classified as an existing type, so be it.

The idea is for our system to conform to our yearnings rather than us trying to conform to the specific tenets of an existing model.

The key emphasis must be on what works for Nigeria not what classification Nigeria can fit into.

CHAPTER NINE

A CONSTITUTION OF AUTONOMOUS AND EQUAL STAKE HOLDERS

*It is unreasonable to expect that equality means that we should
have equal pockets but it is not unreasonable to expect that equality
means that we should have equal say*

As INDICATED EARLIER, NIGERIA'S BIGGEST problem lies in the fact
that its multitudes of ethnic subparts are engaged in a merciless
and trustless competition against one another to take control of
the political center stage.

No ethnic group in Nigeria wants to take marching orders
from the other and none wants to play the second fiddle in the
winner-take-all atmosphere of Nigeria's political theatre.

Each ethnic group wants to be relevant and each wants to
be "*the force*" to reckon with or the "*happening*" ethnic group in
Nigeria. None wants to be dictated to or overshadowed or denied
access to power.

Because of this, Nigeria cannot sustain. The national center stage is too small to withstand the fistful tussle of ethnic interests and unless something drastic is done and quickly, Nigeria will descend into the kind of anarchy and conflagration and mayhem that would make places like Somalia and Sudan look like havens of peace and stability.

Our new constitution must therefore find a way to give each ethnic group the chance to be their own boss, to personally direct and steer the course of their ethnic destiny.

In essence, the constitution must give autonomy and require joint participation at the same time.

Each ethnic group must be capable of directing its own affairs freely and be bound to Nigeria at the same time.

Each ethnic center must be capable of governing itself and yet owe allegiance and good faith to the nation at the same time.

Each ethnic center must be its own boss in most respects and yet be subservient to the nation in some respects at the same time.

The only way to achieve this is to dismantle and dissolve the all-powerful national center stage and to devolve and distribute the immense powers the federal government currently exercises to the states which by their geographic and structural make-up effectively represent the various ethnic centers.

The federal system as it is currently mandated by Nigeria's constitution concentrates all powers in an all-powerful federal government and merely gives cognizance to Nigeria's various ethnic interests on paper. It does not go to any significant extent to empower them.

The new constitution must therefore sufficiently empower the ethnic centers in their home turf and make the national stage less attractive so that it would not matter much who is in control at the national stage.

Devolution of powers to the states would mean that each state would be better positioned to cater more directly to the needs and aspirations of its people in line with their ethnic and cultural values and realities.

Already, the 36-state structure reasonably concentrates people of similar cultures and ethnicities within the same geo-political units. All we need do now is to de-concentrate the powers that the federal government in Nigeria now exercises and empower them.

This would give greater autonomy to the states so that a person in a far-flung place from Abuja like Obubra in Cross River State will not have to look to Abuja for his or her daily survival.

The template of governance that suggests that if Abuja refuses to act, a person in Aghalokpe in Delta State will suffer hardship is egregious and should not be allowed to continue.

To better appreciate what is suggested here, cast back to the time not long ago in the 1960's when we had three and then four regional governments in Nigeria.

The regions; Eastern, Midwestern, Northern, and Western, each comprised of ethnic nationalities with close cultural and social affinities with similar set of objectives.

At that time, the trajectory of progress for the regions and by extension, the individual ethnic nationalities and Nigeria as a whole was promising.

Each region had the necessary autonomy and wherewithal to pursue economic and structural initiatives that paved the way for economic growth and prosperity for its people which in turn had positive implications for Nigeria as a whole.

The only real reason General Gowon dismantled the old four-region structure in the wake of the civil war in 1967 was so that the federal military government could exert more powers and authority over the country.

From then on, we imbibed the culture of absolute authority at the national center and the federal government became a powerful, larger-than-life monolith which controlled everything in the country.

Unfortunately this has remained the case both during our military dictatorships and our civilian democracy.

The only good that has come out of the break up of the old regions is that we now have thirty-six states rather than four large regions which should mean that government ought to be closer to the people than before.

The only problem today is that the 36 governmental units are mere extensions of the federal government without significant powers of their own comparable to the powers the four regions once had.

This has considerably slowed growth and development, tempered individual pursuit and aspiration and has engendered a situation whereby every Nigerian is dependent upon the federal government for even the most basic of necessities.

It has also fostered the competing interests on the national stage today and further alienated grassroots people from government and governance.

The federal system in place in Nigeria today is a military creation because it is a system that is suited perfectly for a military dictatorship which must necessarily exert control from the center.

The federal system has worked in many other countries in

the Western hemisphere such as Canada and France and Britain because they are homogeneous societies.

It has failed to work for a democratic Nigeria because Nigeria much like many other African countries where problems like Nigeria's persists is not a cohesive unit with one common purpose and common agenda.

The new Nigerian constitution must guarantee autonomy and viability to each of its ethnic centers and must treat each ethnic group as an equal partner with equal stakes and equal responsibilities to the nation.

Nigeria can be a strong single-purpose country only if its component parts are individually strong.

Nigeria will become a great country only if its component parts can once more feel a sense of belonging and participation.

Nigerians everywhere will once again have a sense of country only when they can feel that they are a part of an ethnic grouping that is an equal partner in the national scheme.

CHAPTER TEN

THE NECESSITY OF A FOURTH TIER OF GOVERNMENT

The people are a necessary ingredient of a government of the people by the people and for the people

THE SINGLE MOST IMPORTANT AND most significant strand of the kind of transformation that Nigeria needs to become a truly functional democracy and to make the country work for all Nigerians is the creation of a fourth tier of government at the village or autonomous community level.

As a structural imperative, more power should devolve from the center to the states and to smaller governmental units beyond the local government level to effectuate a more dynamic democratic process and to ensure that many more people get directly the benefits of democracy.

Concentration of powers at the national center has tended to alienate the ordinary people from governance and made political office holders distant and disconnected from the people they are supposed to represent.

The present three-tier system; Federal, State and LGA's have not worked effectively well for the Nigerian people and for the country as a whole and should be expanded to ensure wider participation of the people in their governance.

The success of Nigeria's federal system or the emergence of effective and efficient governance in Nigeria greatly depends on an appropriate division of responsibilities and resources between federal, state and local authorities supported by sufficient institutional capacities at each of these levels to carry out their respective assigned functions.

Perhaps, one of the most significant aspects of the colonial system in Nigeria was that Britain adopted a bottom-up approach to governance in which it utilized existing traditional institutions as a foundation for a wider and more effective centralized administration of the country.

Britain recognized early on that the best way to manage its colonial territory was to utilize the people. It knew that the best and most efficient way of building a sustainable colonial regime was to engage the people at their ethnic centers.

The colonial power also recognized the need early in the game to make its presence as the power of the day felt across its colonial territory and took its authority directly to the people.

It corralled the existing traditional and kingship institutions to its advantage and in areas where those institutions did not exist created a warrant chief system that ensured that it maintained an effective control of the territory.

The result is that by the early 1900s, people in even the remotest part of the territory were sufficiently aware of the existence of British might.

And by the dawn of amalgamation in 1914, Britain had effectively entrenched itself within the Nigerian peoples' psyche and for a long time afterwards the influence and effect of governance was much closer to the people and could be felt in every nook and cranny of the country.

Because government and governance were closer to the people, it was possible for the people to feel that governance was all about them. It was also easy for people to pay attention to the goings-on in the government and monitored closely the activities of their appointed or elected officials.

During this period, government officials were more accountable to the people and were conscious and cautious about conducts that they knew would tarnish their reputations and call to question their commitments to service.

The bottom-up system became a crucial part and parcel of an independent Nigeria as the component regions exercised more powers than the federal government and maintained an influential and powerful traditional institutions base.

This had the effect of having the people engaged as well as ensuring that they participated in the politics of their local enclaves.

It is worthy to note that during this period also, the country witnessed its best years politically, economically and agriculturally as empowered, each region took the responsibility of ensuring growth and development within their individual abodes.

The system continued until the collapse of the first republic and was completely sundered by the military's incursion into governance in the mid to late sixties.

Through the military, Nigeria adopted a top-down approach to governance and since then, government and governance has grown farther and further away from the people.

As government and governance grew more and more distant from the ordinary people, government officials no longer felt themselves obligated to selfless service and the result is an explosion of corruption and untoward conduct in public service.

The military-style Unitarian approach in which all authority disseminates from the top further concentrated powers at the national center; stripped the regions of control of economic and political machineries, disemboweled ethnic consciousness within ethnic enclaves and rendered traditional institutions kaput and irrelevant.

While the bottom-up approach created an atmosphere in which each region and by extension each ethnic enclave engaged in a healthy competition to develop and build their respective regions, the top-down approach engendered a situation where the ethnic enclaves were engaged in a competition to seize control of the national center. In order words, the focus changed from what would be good for most of the people to what would be good for a few of the people.

The LGA system was begun in 1976 under the military regime of Generals Murtala Mohammed/ Olusegun Obasanjo and was intended as a mechanism of re-engaging the people and getting them to participate in their governance.

However, while the military was willing to create lower level government centers, it did not adequately empower them to function in a way to bring actual governmental benefits to the people. In order words, power has not necessarily devolved to the people merely with the creation of more local government areas.

Over the years various governments in Nigeria have tended to solve the problem by splitting up local government areas to create more but no matter how many more are created, unless the structure of power distribution is radically redefined, a situation where the people are not adequately engaged would continue to exist.

The three-tier government structure in place in Nigeria today is untenable. The central government controls everything; the states are mere extensions of the national government without any clear sense of political or economic autonomy; and the LGAs are mere paper classifications that are wholly dependent on handouts from the national government.

Real authority can only reside with the people when their state and local governments are given real authorities.

Until the ordinary man in the remote corners of Nigeria can stop relying on the goodwill of the federal government and until he can be sure that he can have a direct say in the policies that affect him, democracy in Nigeria would continue to mean nothing to him.

Nigeria and Nigerians would benefit immensely if the power structure is radically redefined and if smaller governmental units are created to bring governance closer to the people.

Thankfully the traditional institutions upon which the fourth tier of government can be built still exist in Nigeria.

These traditional institutions have little relevance today and have mostly been used by politicians as glorified stooge-fronts and fancy influence-peddlers to undermine and exploit the people.

At the village and autonomous community levels across the country there still exists vibrant political and administrative systems in the form of village assemblies through which local customs are enforced and local tasks such as clearing bushes and cleaning overgrown paths, streams and rivers are performed.

Many communities across Nigeria maintain highly organized and efficient accountability systems such as fines and penalty impositions for customs violations and local vigilante groups to provide security. In many instances these communities coordinate with local law enforcement agencies to maintain peace and order.

The difference between what exists now and what is proposed here is that today, the communities and villages have no authority to do what they are doing.

The tasks they perform are not mandatory and the fines they impose are actually illegal under Nigerian law.

They have no power to enforce their customs and they cannot demand compliance from members of their communities. They have to rely on the willing submission of people to any required code of conduct.

I recently attended a village meeting where two neighboring landowners presented a small dispute about who owned a plantain tree on the boundary of their lands.

Although the meeting heard both their arguments and returned a verdict in favor of one of the landowners, the losing landowner swore that he would not comply with the decision. In that situation, there was nothing further the meeting could do. Unless the loser complied with their decision in good faith, their decision had no effect.

Consider what the situation would be if the village meeting had some teeth by way of legal authority to adjudicate and resolve issues such as the plantain tree dispute.

There would be an efficient system of checks and balances

at that fundamental level that would in turn have far reaching impact on the overall polity of the country.

The necessity of a fourth tier of government in Nigeria cannot be overemphasized. Apart from bringing governance with real and actual authority closer to the people, it would help foster growth, ensure greater autonomy and engender less dependence on the national center.

To get a better sense of the point being made here, consider an experimental family of six children who have been given various amounts of money with which to pursue their goals.

Which of the following scenarios would better ensure that they are a more formidable and more prosperous family?

One, a situation where they have put their monies in a common pool and all lived together with their wives and children in a huge multi-roomed house where resources and privileges are shared.

Or two, a situation in which each child and his family lived in separate households according to their individual strengths and capacities.

Nigeria today is analogous to the six families living in the same household. No matter how much resources and privileges there are and no matter how organized the household is, there is bound to be some friction in their relationships and there is bound to be people who would get a better deal than the others just because they are better at scheming and manipulation.

What is proposed here is analogous to the six families living in separate households. Each child has the unique opportunity of determining what is good for his family without consideration of what his siblings might think.

Each is able to more effectively control his resources and decide without interference about how to apply or utilize them.

This option permits each person to pursue his interests to the best of his ability and offers the best hope for focused pursuit and self realization.

Empowering the ordinary Nigerian in his local homestead by giving him a more direct access to a government in which he has vested interest is the best way of re-engaging Nigerians in the well-being of their communities and by extension, the well-being of Nigeria.

Creating a fourth tier of government at the village or autonomous community level is the best way of de-emphasizing the hustle and tussle at the national center and to ensure a more focused growth and development at the local and regional level.

CHAPTER ELEVEN

PORTRAIT OF A FOUR-TIERED NIGERIA

Government ought to be about ensuring the basic needs of most; not assuring the expensive tastes of a few

ESSENTIAL TO THE CREATION OF a fourth tier of government in Nigeria is the dismantling of the present power structure that is lopsided in favor of the federal government and devolution of powers from the national center to the states.

The present federal government is too big and too powerful and this promotes a winner-take-all mentality among the competing ethnic and political interests and engenders an atmosphere in which political office holders use the apparatuses of government for their personal interests rather than the collective interests of all Nigerians.

Because everybody in Nigeria is focused on Abuja and the titillations of political power and influence at the center, emphasis is more on what people could get out of the country rather than on the basic things that would set the country on a path to sustainable growth.

In the twelve or so years of Nigeria's present democracy there is hardly any significant progress that has been made to improve the overall well-being of Nigerians.

A cursory look at the legislative accomplishments of the democratic era from 1999 to the present shows that Nigeria's law makers have not made any significant legislative enactments aimed at improving democratic governance in the country.

A majority of legislative achievements have been in the areas that either benefit the legislators personally or advance their personal as well as narrow group interests. Most of the debate has focused on who should control what resources and who should exercise which power over what sectors.

In reality, the federal government in Nigeria has mainly been all about power tussles and influence peddling as well as assuring the expensive tastes and habits of a few well-connected people rather than ensuring the basic needs of ordinary Nigerians.

A much narrower and more specific legislative and executive agenda that would drastically cut down on the number of items on the executive and legislatives lists would have the effect of engendering a more focused government.

In the new four-tier dispensation, the power sharing scheme must radically whittle down the powers and influence of the federal government. The federal government's exercise of power would be roughly 20-30% while 70-80% is shared between the states, LGAs and village governments.

Under the new dispensation, the federal government would be smaller and perform core traditional tasks such as national defense and maintaining a national army, foreign affairs and international matters, taxation, interstate arbitration and regulation of matters between the states.

The federal government would maintain national law enforcement agencies for national law enforcement and national regulatory agencies for national and interstate regulatory purposes. There would be a federal police and federal intelligence agencies which purposes are limited to interstate law enforcement and peace keeping.

It would maintain a federal three-tier judiciary system consisting of a Supreme Court, regional Appeal Courts and District or Zonal Courts for federal constitutional matters, interstate matters and disputes, etc.

It would also maintain special and administrative courts at the district or zonal level for matters outside the purview of regular courts such as bankruptcy, maritime, tax, etc.

The federal government would also retain control and regulation of oil and other natural resources to ensure unity and establish an effective and efficient allocation and distribution formula for proceeds from natural resources to ensure equity.

There would be dual tax regimes for federal government and states and institution of strong tax enforcement policies.

At the state level, most government business has focused mainly on maintaining large bureaucracies and paying salaries to millions of redundant and unproductive government personnel.

Most states in Nigeria have very little to show by way of development and growth and majority of them have only one source of revenue; the monthly allocations from the federal government.

Under the new dispensation, each state would be governed by a state constitution and states would have control of core administrative, social, political and economic tasks and be sufficiently empowered to create a mechanism for promoting private enterprise, local industrial development and economic growth.

There would be states law enforcement agencies for intra-state law enforcement and states regulatory agencies for intra-state regulatory purposes.

There would be a state police and state investigative and intelligence agencies which purposes are limited to state law enforcement and peace keeping.

There would be state three-tier judiciary system consisting of a state Supreme Court, Appeal Courts, and Municipal or Local government Courts for intrastate issues and local disputes, etc.

Conduct of elections would be the exclusive preserve of states, local governments and village governments with the village government having the prerequisite to conduct elections.

At the current LGA level, chairmen and councilors sit around doing nothing much of the time.

When they receive their monthly allocations from the federal government, they share it amongst themselves and their cronies and then sit back and await the next disbursement.

Because most communities rely on self-help projects which they fund through project launchings, fund raisers and donations from illustrious members of the communities, the LGAs have little to show for the revenues they collect monthly from the federal government. Because of this also, corruption thrives and the elected officials pocket monies that should go to developing cottage industries that would translate to economic empowerment of the people.

Although the fourth schedule of the present Nigerian

constitution mandates certain tasks for the LGAs to perform, in practice most LGA administrations in Nigeria have no idea what they are required to do or pretend that they do not have enough resources to carry out their functions. In most of them, the only task they perform is to pay salaries to their employees.

In the proposed new dispensation, the role of the local government area would be a little more specific and direct and rather than being under the control of the state assembly as required by the constitution, they would exercise a level of autonomy that would permit them to do the things that actually benefit the people.

At the LGA level, there would be an elected board of directors who would manage the affairs of the LGA and employ the necessary work force to carry out its assigned tasks.

Each LGA would be required to allocate resources in its budget for the creation and completion of at least one cottage industry per year or the execution of a capital project within its administrative area. In so doing, development and employment opportunities would come readily to the citizens of the LGA.

At the village or autonomous community level, existing village council structures would be adopted as a template for village administration.

Each village government center would receive allocation from the federal government based on a revised and expanded allocation formula and there would be an elected village administration and council that mirrors in a smaller sense both LGA and state government structures.

Village governments would be administered by village ordinances that reflect the spirit and tenor of state and federal laws and each village government would have and manage its own independent village police to provide law enforcement in order to enhance security.

There would be established, a structure of law enforcement cooperation and mutuality between different levels of police; village, LGA, state, and federal with independent federal and state level police service commissions or oversight commissions to regulate police conduct and affairs.

For an efficient and effective four-tier structure to function in Nigeria drastic changes would have to be made in the manner other businesses of government are conducted.

Most crucial is the elections and electoral process. The current electoral system in which an-all powerful INEC chairman has the final say in what results to publish is not tenable and should be abolished and supplanted with a system that ensures the integrity of elections and the electoral process.

Conduct of elections in the new dispensation should be the exclusive preserve of local governments and village administrations.

Every village administration should have the capacity to conduct and certify election results in their jurisdiction and have copies of the results available for inspection by any member of the public.

This would allow for greater accountability and would make it difficult for anyone to alter the results from a village.

By this mechanism also election results will be readily ascertainable once elections are over. Successful candidates at village level will be known right away. The village board will then report results to LGA for collation with results from other villages at which point LGA level results will be published and so on and so forth.

There would be independent federal, state and LGA election boards to function only as collation points for national, state-wide or regional election results respectively.

Another important structural imperative for the success of the four-tier governmental structure is reform in the way infrastructure development and economic autonomy is characterized.

There should not be anything limiting how village and local governments apply their resources in order to promote economic growth and to build the necessary infrastructure for their communities.

Village governments should be free to build roads and water projects without approval of state and local governments except where doing so would impinge on their rights and obligations.

Village and local governments should have the ability to create the necessary incentives to attract private or corporate investments and to draw any benefits arising thereof.

Private or corporate interests would be permitted to invest in electricity generation and supply with the federal government's role strictly limited to regulation and oversight.

There would be collaboration between the states and federal government on construction projects within states' territory and state governments will be required to oversee federal contracts for construction projects in their territory. This would promote greater accountability because states have incentive to ensure that projects are completed as required and according to specifications.

In the public service sector, there is a need to scrap the federal character reflecting system of balancing employment of public officials as enshrined in the current constitution because it does not promote excellence and efficiency. A system based on merits, qualification, competence and performance should be instituted.

Instituting a transparent recruiting system rather than employing one based on quota system would ensure public accountability and a more efficient civil service. Public establishments would be required to maintain records of recruitment or hiring exercises which will be available for public scrutiny.

For a smooth flow of the public service labor force, discrimination and nepotism laws would need to be enhanced to discourage acts of discrimination and favoritism.

Also paramount to the success of the four-tier system is the installation of modern technology capabilities at every level of government and in every public sector. Records keeping and data management is a highly efficient mechanism of staving off corruption and illicit practices.

Nigeria has the wherewithal to install and manage effective technologies that would make for a smooth and convenient operation of government.

The millions of naira and dollars that are looted from government coffers on a yearly basis are sufficient to equip Nigeria with the necessary technological resources to make it work for every Nigerian.

The essence of the fourth tier is not to create another level of government to mirror the corruption and rot in the existing levels of government.

The essence is to dilute and distribute governance and to make government more compact and effective and less like a multi-faceted and counterproductive entity.

With smaller government structures that are empowered to perform significant functions, it would be easier for people to keep an eye on how the resources available to their community governments are applied and utilized.

Imagine how impossible it would be for a village official to embezzle or steal funds under the watchful eyes of members of his community. They have known him all their lives and it would be easy for them to tell the source of any wealth he flaunts.

Instituting a fourth tier of government is Nigeria's best chance of defusing the overarching influence of the federal government and would give the ordinary peoples of Nigeria the best opportunity of building a community and country that works for their interests and not the interest of a few powerful people.

CHAPTER TWELVE

MANAGING NIGERIA'S NATURAL WEALTH

Oil may belong to all, but some people suffer more because of it

OIL, THE MAINSTAY OF NIGERIA'S economy and the only reason Nigeria is viable as a country is also Nigeria's biggest headache.

It is the only thing that has kept Nigeria together as one country and the one sure thing that would rend it.

Perhaps the most contentious issues about oil in Nigeria are; how to characterize ownership rights? Who should have control over it? How the revenues derived from it should be distributed? Whether it is appropriate that wealth produced from one part of the country should be used to develop and build other parts of the country?

The answers to how to characterize the ownership rights to and who should have control of Nigeria's oil and any other naturally occurring resource for that matter irrespective of where the resource is located is simple.

There is no question, the ownership rights belong to all

Nigerians and by implication control is vested in the government of Nigeria.

The argument that Nigeria's oil wealth should be owned and controlled by the people from whose land it is milked is lame and fails to take into consideration the fact that before oil, there was Nigeria.

Unfortunately for those who hanker for control of oil by those who produce it, the moment Nigeria became a single political entity, it, by implication became the owner of all the lands and territories and the resources within its geographical definition.

It is foolhardy therefore to assume that because the country's wealth is produced in one region, it cannot be used to develop another. Unfortunately, it is the same argument that a person from a non-oil producing part of say Rivers state makes about his entitlement to the proceeds from oil that a person in say Borno state can make.

The oil does not belong to a person from a non-oil producing community in the south of Nigeria any more than it belongs to a person from a non-oil producing community in the north of Nigeria.

However, there is a wide yawn of injustice and impropriety with respect to how the oil wealth is distributed.

There is a valid point in the assertion by agitators that the people who are impacted directly by the exploitation of any naturally occurring resource should be treated differently from those who are not directly impacted.

It makes perfect sense that the people directly affected should get a better deal and enjoy greater benefits than those who are far-flung from the fields from which the resource is produced.

Oil was first discovered at Oloibiri, near Port Harcourt in 1958 and became the life blood of Nigeria during the international oil market boom of the early 70s.

Since then the vast network of mangrove swamps in Nigeria's Niger Delta, possibly the largest wetlands in the world, has been producing oil and billions of dollars in revenue for the government of Nigeria and foreign oil companies while the local folks from whose land the oil is milked live in utter misery and sheer poverty.

With massive exploitation of oil and endless deluge of hard revenues for the country, every other natural resource such as tin, coal and an innumerable host of others from which Nigeria could have derived immeasurable wealth were abandoned or completely forgotten or relegated to irrelevance.

With the vast oil wealth came the scourge of corruption and open-eyed thievery tilted to the advantage of the powerful and influential resulting in huge disparities in wealth and economic well-being between the haves and the haves-not.

The injustices suffered by the folks who have been directly impacted by oil exploitation and wealth production in time spurned spasms of agitation and outcry by groups such as Movement for the Survival of Ogoni People (MOSOP) spearheaded by the dexterious Ken Saro Wiwa and Movement for the Emancipation of the Niger Delta (MEND) a loose network of angry and disadvantaged young people from the Niger-Delta.

MOSOP and MEND have sought to wrest their just due from the exploitation of their land and insist on local control of oil resources, but that has remained more of a tall dream than an achievable goal.

One of the unfortunate outcomes of the discovery of oil in Nigeria and its emergence as the primal natural resource and paramount wealth producing item in Nigeria is how to define and characterize its ownership and whether there is an inherent right to a larger stake in the wealth it produces with respect to those from whose land it is milked.

To the person in the oil producing community or state or local government area, the oil belongs to him and he has a strong feeling that he should be allowed to control the oil and to decide who gets benefits out of it and who does not.

To the person up north who is far removed from the drilling fields and exploration grounds, the oil belongs to all of Nigeria and he has a strong sentiment that he should derive as much benefits from the wealth it produces as the person from whose backyard it is milked.

However, there are certain realities that many of the policies that various governments in Nigeria have pursued over the years have failed to take into consideration with regards to how oil exploitation is characterized and how oil wealth is distributed.

The most crucial of these realities is that beyond the oil producing community or local government area or state or region, there is the individual, a human being, a person.

Indeed every policy has tended to ignore the bare-faced fact that behind every naira and kobo or dollar and cent that oil has generated in Nigeria, there is a person; a Mr. Opobo or Mr. Ogoni or Mr. Bonny who has been directly and personally affected or impacted by the exploitation of oil.

Each policy has tended to treat the individual as a non-entity and presumes that his significant interest must inexplicably be tied to his community or to his state.

As is typical of every Nigerian policy construct, the well-being and interests of the individual is oftentimes lost in simplistic tribal classifications and facile group characterizations.

Sadly, successive policies on distribution of wealth from oil production have failed to recognize the reality that in the hierarchical ladder of distribution, the smallest and most important unit of classification is the individual and not his village or LGA or state.

In the same vein groups such as MOSOP and MEND have imbibed the notion of group agitation for group interests rather than group agitation for individual interest.

This is why all the policies applied so far have consistently failed to engender a tranquil environment for the smooth and progressive exploitation of oil. It is also why agitations by MOSOP and MEND have not yielded any real benefits.

The single most significant strand of any reform agenda must therefore take into consideration the reality of the individual.

It is the individual who is in the first line of attack and therefore should matter most in the scheme of things especially in the distribution of oil wealth in Nigeria and in every other aspect of Nigerian life.

The pattern of glossing over the individual is wholly unfair and sardonic and should forthwith be done away with.

The individual in the oil-producing areas of Nigeria should be the first unit of consideration before his village or his LGA or his state or a person far flung from the producing fields.

The interest of the individual should take priority even over the interests of Nigeria because before the first dime from oil drops, he is the person who loses his land, his livelihood and his inheritance.

The consideration of how oil wealth should be distributed

should begin from this individual because before there is a collective impact, there is an individual impact and before there is a collective loss, there is an individual loss.

Such consideration should not therefore begin from a collective standpoint as is the present case in Nigeria because it tends to not directly address the significant interest and aspirations of the individual who has to live with the nightmare of resource production.

The present derivation formula used in distributing oil wealth in Nigeria is wantonly unfair because it presumes that every person in an oil producing state like say, Rivers State, should get an equal shrift and should be treated as one wealth-producing entity.

The biggest problem with the present derivation formula is that it does not put the wealth in the hands of those who are entitled to it.

The most viable way to distribute wealth from natural resources in Nigeria is to factor in the individual who is directly impacted in the scheme of distribution by way of providing for special compensation for land, livelihood and relocation.

The same distribution scheme should also be applied to every other natural resource in Nigeria. This would have the effect of encouraging the exploitation of other natural resources across Nigeria and greatly expand the revenue base of the country as a whole.

A simple distribution scheme would take the following format: Natural resource producing states earn a taxed percentage of earnings. Natural resource producing communities earn a taxed percentage of resource earnings. Special individualized royalty or compensation funds for persons directly impacted by natural resource production.

If directly impacted by oil or other natural resource production, an individual is entitled to a percentage of earnings attributable to his appropriated land or facility and whatever funds that he is entitled to should be paid directly to him rather than funneled through some ineffective ombudsman organization.

This is the best method of ensuring that persons directly affected by resource production will receive their just compensation and help promote an overall atmosphere in which some people would not feel shortchanged and resort to violence and militancy in order to secure their just due.

PART III

PATHWAYS TO CHANGE

CHAPTER THIRTEEN

LEADERSHIP INITIATIVES FOR SWEEPING REFORMS IN NIGERIA

Change rarely comes out of the benevolence and magnanimity of those against whom the wind of change will blow

CHANGE, NO MATTER WHAT KIND, has never come easy. However change is always inevitable in the face of persistent and vibrant advocacy. Also change rarely comes out of the benevolence and magnanimity of those against whom the wind of change will blow.

The kinds of sweeping reforms which will take Nigeria to a new place where every Nigerian would experience the full benefit of a prosperous and dynamic democratic state would require drastic and committed action.

It will indeed be very challenging and difficult to upend the applecart of the status quo from which a few powerful and influential people benefit, but there are possibilities.

The first possibility would require the effort of the present political leadership in Nigeria.

This means that they would have to come to their senses and voluntarily awaken to the reality that a situation where a few people grab for themselves the goodies that belongs to all cannot be sustained for much longer and that the country faces a peril of disintegrating into utter chaos and lawlessness unless something urgent is done.

The second possibility would require the effort of ordinary Nigerians who must awaken from their complacency and agitate for sweeping reforms in order to save their country or face the ugly possibility that they would soon not have a country they could call their own much less one they could be proud of.

In the event that the political leadership will not voluntarily bring about change, the people would have to force their hand through the kind of revolutions that have swept through many countries in recent years; the ordinary people's revolution.

The first possibility presupposes that the entire political leadership must come to their senses and do the right thing. This is a tall hope because nowhere else in history have those who benefit from the spoils of a dysfunctional and corrupt government willingly and voluntarily embraced reform.

To expect that the caliber of politicians we have in Nigeria today are capable of voluntarily reforming Nigeria so that it works for every Nigerian and not just for the well-connected politician is indeed farfetched, but it is not entirely fortuitous to hold out hope for such a possibility.

To begin with, the president along with members of Nigeria's national assembly must come to terms with the fact that the entire Nigerian political, economic and social structures have to be dismantled and rebuilt from scratch.

To set the stage for reforms, the president in concert with the national assembly must appoint panels of experts from different fields of endeavor and charge them with a complete rewrite of the playbook of every sector and aspect of Nigeria.

These panels do not have to be multi-member panels. Each panel should have at the most, three members and more importantly, the panels do not have to necessarily reflect the ethnic profile of the country.

The simple charge to each panel would be to come up with not just recommendations, but brand new templates by which every aspect of the country would be reorganized.

One of the pitfalls of constituting panels or committees to solve problems in Nigeria is that there is always a conscious and concerted effort to ensure that every ethnic group in Nigeria is represented in any panel or committee. This has tended to make them look more like a negotiation of rights and interests between the ethnicities rather than meeting of minds to articulate and solve the problems at hand.

In the past, too much emphasis is placed in the composition and make-up of panel membership that by the time a typical panel gets down to work, its purpose is already undermined or diminished by an argument about who should be in the panel and who should not.

We must get away from the notion that for a sound policy to be formulated in Nigeria every ethnic interest must pitch in or every ethnic opinion has to be expressed.

The problem with Nigeria is not that the opinion of every ethnic group is not represented in the way policies are formulated. Solving Nigeria's problems does not necessarily require input by every ethnic group. Solving Nigeria's problems must therefore be ethnicity-neutral.

Also, we do not need a bunch of people to create a sound policy and we certainly do not need every person to be at the table in order to develop a policy that will work for everybody.

A significant stumbling block to implementing this kind of leadership initiative is that there is no existing constitutional standpoint from which to do so.

The present constitution neither provides a mandate nor prescribes a path for this kind of action and it is expected that those who would resist the idea would argue that it is unconstitutional.

In other words, the constitution arrogates to itself supreme authority without providing for a means of abrogating those powers or voiding its authority.

It does however provide for how the powers can be tinkered with or tweaked. Unfortunately, as explained earlier, it would require a lengthy exercise and take a massive amount of tweaking and tinkering to make it right and Nigeria cannot afford that.

In taking this initiative, the political leadership should not therefore look to the present constitution for authority to do so. The measure can be achieved through the use of a public referendum or plebiscite so that the Nigerian people would decide on the way forward.

There has to be a panel or committee for everything. Each panel will not just tweak and adjust the existing systems and policies; each panel would have to rethink and conceive a brand new system that is guaranteed to be effective and efficient.

CONSTITUTION

The constitution redo committee will be charged with the task of producing an entirely new constitution that is specifically tailored to the needs of Nigeria.

The new constitution must focus on the individual and define as its central purpose the protection of the rights and aspirations of the individual and the promotion of the rule of law.

It must redefine Nigeria as a nation of individuals rather than as a nation of ethnicities, grant sufficient autonomy to the component states and establish a four-tier government system that would ensure that governance is closer to the people.

The constitution must limit the powers of the federal government to core traditional tasks and devolve bulk of the powers and control over matters such as elections, business licensing and registration, education, the police, crime and prosecution, etc to the states.

It must whittle down considerably the laundry list of items in the federal executive and federal legislative lists in the current constitution in order to ensure that the federal government does not have too much control over the affairs of the people.

Above all else, the new constitution must be written in an easy to read and easy to comprehend language and must not be riddled with conflicting notions and provisions.

PUBLIC SERVICE

There should be a committee to rethink and reconfigure Nigeria's public service with a view to dismantling all the bureaucratic structures that make it possible for corruption to thrive. One of the principal focuses will be to ensure that no one person has super control over public resources or decision making processes.

A chief task of the public sector reform committee will be to work into the fabric of the new system an effective mechanism of checks and balances such as efficient electronic record keeping, data management, transparency, and oversight.

The false notion of federal character has to be done away with to ensure that only competent and qualified persons are employed in the country's public service.

Since the states under the new deal would exercise more powers and have control over a broad range of issues the federal government would be smaller and less attractive and therefore would not attract the kind of unhealthy and unnecessary competition to secure employment with the federal government that has plagued public employment for decades.

ELECTORAL POLICY

There should be a committee to rethink and produce a brand new electoral policy that ensures that states rather than the federal government are charged with the task of conducting elections.

Because all politics is local and because all the elective offices are essentially at the states' level, it makes sense to have each state conduct elections. There will not be any need for a national electoral commission and a situation where politicians look to an all-powerful federal electoral official to manipulate results will become a thing of the past.

There is no overstating the need for comprehensive electoral reforms in Nigeria. The making of the corrupt politician begins long before the elections but the making of the systemic pillage of the nation's coffers begins at the elections.

Politicians stake everything to gain control of office. There are no control mechanisms to check the excesses of politicians and their supporters and cohorts. The electoral commission is nothing but an extension of the party in power. There's no guarantee that the votes cast will be the votes counted. Election results are known even before the voting is over. At the end of the day, political office holders do not consider themselves accountable to anyone but themselves.

No one doubts that the electoral system in Nigeria is horrible and everyone it does appear agrees that the system needs fixing.

One of the most troubling aspects of Nigeria's eleven year-old democracy is the sad reality that it has become a one-party state in many respects especially at the national level. The choices available to people have grown more and more narrow and uncompetitive. There is no justification for the party in power at any level to use its incumbency and control over the electoral process to thwart the will of the people.

Reform will embrace every aspect of Nigeria's electoral process including complete and true independence of electoral commissions at the states' level, electronic voting, and curbing the excesses of politicians and political stalwarts. Due consideration should also be given to instituting a one-term political office tenures in order to limit abuse of incumbent powers and one party control.

LEGAL SYSTEM

There should be a committee to rethink and restructure Nigeria's legal system, the operation of rule of law and the judiciary.

Our laws should give us order and comfort and hold us accountable for our actions. No one person should be above them. Not even the mightiest politician or the most highly connected person.

Corruption thrives in Nigeria because there is no effective mechanism for holding people accountable.

It is hard to imagine that there are laws in Nigeria which make bribery and corruption and embezzlement of public funds very serious criminal offences that mandate tough prison sentences.

Yet people behave as if there is absolutely nothing wrong with paying bribes and illegal up-front fees. The laws should be strengthened and efficient mechanisms for their enforcement put in place to achieve deterrence and punishment.

There should be equal protection under the laws in practice and not in theory and no person should be above the law. A system in which people are given the necessary incentives by way of reward to report on corrupt practices should be top priority.

Nigeria's legal system is a patchwork of courts of various jurisdictions but of very little positive impact on ordinary Nigerians.

Only the well-connected and the rich benefit from the current legal system in Nigeria. The poor and less privileged are at the mercy of the police who oftentimes double as judge and prosecutor.

Security is laughable because of a police force that is underpaid, poorly trained and subsumed in corruption. Control of the entire police is in the hands of the president in Abuja. Governors who want to be in the good books of the police have to be suppliant to the president.

Reforming the legal system would mean instituting mechanisms for ensuring the independence of the judiciary by creating parallel states court systems.

Reforming the security system would include breaking the centralized command structure of the police by permitting the creation of states' police forces and raising the prerequisites for admitting people into the force.

A well-educated, well paid, technologically savvy and well equipped police force should be a top priority goal.

EDUCATION

There should be a committee to rethink and restructure Nigeria's education system.

Education policies in the current dispensation are in disarray and are not geared towards a uniform education agenda for the country.

The academic curricula used to be standardized around the country. Now, there is no cohesive educational plan for Nigeria. It is now every educational institution for itself especially at the foundational and fundamental levels.

Sadly, there is no clear indication of what Nigeria's educational goals are. Most academic institutions are more interested in building lavish structures and collecting massively excessive fees. There is little regulation and there is no guarantee that a person who is flaunting an academic degree has any knowledge or skill to back it up.

Reform in the educational sector would entail once again, streamlining the educational goals of the country with a view to ensuring that Nigeria produces the kinds of educated people that can compete in the ever bourgeoning innovative global stage.

INFRASTRUCTURE

There should be a committee to rethink and restructure Nigeria's infrastructure which despite the billions of dollars the country earns in revenue yearly have continued to deteriorate and in many instances are decrepit or non existent.

There is no reason on earth why Nigeria cannot have the kinds of modern infrastructure that exist in many developed countries around the world. If the billions of dollars Nigeria earns yearly are invested in infrastructure rather than stolen by corrupt government officials, Nigeria would be one of the best places to live in the world.

It is unthinkable that in a country as vast and dynamic as Nigeria, we do not have a working railway transportation system. Rather than improve on structures that were built in the years when corruption was not as widespread, we have become more and more backward even in the most basic things that would make our country better.

Reform must mean curbing corruption in the way contracts for construction projects are awarded and in the way they are executed.

There must be a conscious effort to install a system of checks and oversight that makes it impossible for people to steal funds meant for infrastructure projects.

Reform must also entail opening up the energy sector to private investment without an undue overburdening by the federal government by way of unduly burdensome license fees, huge start-up costs and bureaucratic rigmaroles.

Investors should be free to set up mechanism to produce and market electricity. Market forces would weed out bad and unserious investors and limit the industry to those who are efficient and serious. The role of the government would be limited to regulating the sector by writing rules of the road that would curtail abuses and excesses of industry practitioners.

BOUNDARY LINES

There should be a panel or committee to reassess the boundary lines between communities and states and recommend an efficient system of mapping, documenting and preserving records so that there will not be any question regarding the demarcation lines between communities or states. This would put to rest the incessant instances of boundary disputes which have in recent years become a serious problem amongst Nigerian communities. It is unfortunate that the government has to resort to shipping soldiers to trouble spots to quell disputes rather than resolving boundary disputes by simply pulling up a map from the archives to show who owns what and who does not.

As indicated earlier, the possibility of the corrupt officials and politicians who currently benefit from the system to embrace comprehensive reform ideas is very remote. As we have seen by their actions, they are only interested in the things that benefit their class and not the things that would benefit all Nigerians.

However, this option is Nigeria's best and most-hassle-free option.

In setting its sights on reforming Nigeria for the better, Nigeria's political leadership must have a clear and intelligent idea of what the reform agenda should be.

In the event that they would not voluntarily take on the task with minimum prodding, then it would be up to the people to take appropriate action.

CHAPTER FOURTEEN

BLUEPRINT FOR A PEOPLE'S REVOLUTION IN NIGERIA

A country without a vibrant and vociferous citizenry is a country curst to mediocrity

IN THE EVENT THAT THE political leadership in Nigeria will not come to their senses and not only realize that the way things are going in the country cannot be sustained for much longer but also take drastic actions aimed at setting the country aright, then it will be up to the ordinary people of Nigeria to do something.

However, the idea of a peoples' revolution in Nigeria raises some pertinent questions.

What will it take for ordinary Nigerians to rise to the challenge of redeeming their country from systemic rot, structural stench and the despoliation of their national heritage?

What would it take to rout Nigerians from their complacence and noncommittal attitude towards the vapid and rancorous political wheeling and dealing in their country?

How much worse can things get in their country before Nigerians can go from being armchair bemoaners and critics to revolutionary flag bearers and beckoners of hope and prosperity for their country?

Is it possible to have a peoples' revolution in Nigeria?

Is it possible to have in Nigeria anything close to the kinds of peoples' revolt that have swept through many nations of the world in recent months and in the not-too-distant past?

Someone once posited that the typical Nigerian is so complacent that if he is pushed to the wall, he would simply drill a hole in the wall to create more step-back space rather than fight back.

That it would take more than a catastrophic event in Nigeria's political life to get ordinary Nigerians sufficiently riled up to fight back at a system that is so uneven-handed and lopsided in favor of the political elite that their lives is nothing but recurring misery.

That ordinary Nigerians are much too divided by ethnic notions and religious sentiments to be able to join together to form a unifying agenda for a collective purpose.

That the ordinary Nigerian is more interested in self-preservation and self-gratification than in social equity and collective well being and that he will not sacrifice a drop of sweat for his country's sake.

That the ordinary Nigerian is so much preoccupied with his personal survival and satisfying his aching hunger that asking him to sacrifice his personal convenience for the good of his country is asking him to do the impossible.

It is also true that most Nigerians have grown reticent and weary and indifferent to the thievery and corruption and wanton political wheeling and dealing in their country and have become accepting of it and decided that there is nothing anyone can do about it.

Yes, most Nigerians have no sense of country and yes, most Nigerians would rather sit on the sidelines and complain bitterly and endlessly about the rot and decay in their country rather than lift a finger to do something about it.

The complacence of the ordinary Nigerian is palpable and disheartening to the extent that the old cliché *"a hungry man is an angry man"* no longer rings true in Nigeria.

The hungry Nigerian has imbibed a virtue of resigned quietude. He is resigned to fate and has invested the last vestiges of his hopes in some kind of messianic salvation.

He blames himself for his shortcomings and misgivings and misfortune rather than the system or the self-dealing politician whom he prefers to see as one of the fortunate few upon whom providence has specially chosen to bestow good fortune.

Yes, the ordinary Nigerian, Nigeria's best hope for redemption, has been roundly deflated of verve and energy to the point that he is unwilling to partake in anything that would unsettle his delicate survival equilibrium.

However there are signs that the ordinary Nigerian is not completely defeated. He is down but the count is not out. It is still possible to stir something in him.

With the proper incentive, an ordinary peoples' revolution is very much possible in Nigeria despite the nonchalant and noncommittal attitudinal postures of most Nigerians to the unsavory situation in their country.

What it will take for ordinary Nigerians to rise from near defeat and hopelessness to the challenge of redeeming their country has been with ordinary Nigerians for many decades.

It has festered and seethed and frothed and reached a boiling point and it is now ready to explode.

What it will take is the sheer poverty and desperate hunger that many Nigerians are facing every day while the crooks and highwaymen and carpetbaggers who have hijacked the corridors of political power in their country feast and revel in rabid opulence and obscene wealth.

It is the kinds of sheer deprivation and economic oppression that have left a majority of Nigerians, irrespective of their ethnic or religious affinity, wondering what the future holds for them and for their children and grandchildren.

It is the disillusionment and despair that the promise of a once bountiful homeland in which their dreams could be fulfilled and their aspirations sated has been swept away in the thick murky mist of corruption and kleptomania by the privileged few.

It is the hopelessness and frustration that their homeland of many possibilities has become an Augean stable of dashed hopes and stifled aspirations.

Yes, the ordinary peoples' revolution is possible and ready to happen in Nigeria because ordinary Nigerians have come to a point where they can no longer stand the stench and vile and putrescence in their country.

The ordinary people's revolution is possible and ready to happen in Nigeria because ordinary Nigerians are fed up with the ugly and unfortunate reality that their beloved country is only working for a few people.

The ordinary people's revolution is possible and ready to happen in Nigeria because ordinary Nigerians can no longer bear the hunger and deprivation and frustration of living in a country where the privileged political elite line their pockets with loot while they, the ordinary people live on prayers and empty promises.

However, for a successful peoples' revolution to happen in Nigeria, it has to be well planned, have a clear and specific as well as central purpose and be all-inclusive.

Perhaps the biggest obstacle to a people's revolution in Nigeria is a lack of a sense of collective destiny on the part of ordinary Nigerians which is made much worse by a prevailing atmosphere of ethnic divisiveness, suspiciousness and rivalry. But these can be overcome.

For a peoples' revolution to happen, there needs to be a concerted effort to rally past the prevalent themes of ethnic and religious divisiveness and differences and trump up common interests so that it does not appear that the revolution is tilted in favor of one ethnic group or the other or one religious group or the other.

In short, the people's revolution must be ethnicity and religion blind to succeed.

Those who perpetrate corruption have thrived because they continue to drive and instigate divisive notions of ethnic and religious differences.

They know that it will be impossible for oppressed Nigerians to come together for a common purpose because of the huge gorge of distrust and suspiciousness amongst them.

The task of overcoming ethnocentric and religious sentiments and divisions in order to drive a revolution for a common goal is a daunting task in Nigeria, but it is very possible.

Thankfully, there is a common thread that binds ordinary Nigerians from east to west and from north to south and that is simply the fact that they have suffered the same fate and have been at the losing end of a corrupt and dysfunctional country.

Suffering and economic oppression and subhuman existence does not know ethnicity or religion.

There is no difference between the starvation and suffering of the people in Northern Nigeria and the starvation and suffering of people in Southern Nigeria and likewise there is no difference between the frustration and hopelessness of the people in Eastern Nigeria and the frustration and hopelessness of the people in Western Nigeria.

Similarly, there is no difference between the economic repression of the ordinary Nigerian Moslem and the economic repression of the ordinary Nigerian Christian or any other religion for that matter.

The anxiety and resentment is the same everywhere and this is the core the revolutionary message must tap into.

As long as the revolution can articulate a message and a purpose that is ethnicity and religion neutral and resonates with every Nigerian irrespective of his or her ethnic or religious affinity, there is a good chance that an ordinary peoples' revolution in Nigeria will succeed.

The revolution must not be revolution for revolution's sake. It must not be revolution just because it is fashionable and appealing and trending. It must be revolution because the people have no other choice.

The revolution must be self reliant. It must not depend on the intervention of foreign forces or countries because that would mean that if no help comes, the revolution will die a miserable death.

The messaging must be clear and convincing and the organizing must begin at the grassroots where the pain is most felt. The goal must be national but the strategy must be local.

The goal of the revolution must be to scrap the present systems and structures in place and institute a system of governance that guarantees that the country works for all Nigerians and not a few well-placed Nigerians.

The revolution must define its enemy as the systems and structures in place in Nigeria that make it easy for corruption and other malaises to thrive.

The basic precept of the revolution must be that every Nigerian, including the Nigerian who wears corruption as a vest is a victim.

We are all victims because we have permitted to stand systems and structures that make it easy for corruption and inequity to thrive.

We have erected a national storehouse of treasures and we have continuously entrusted the keys to just one person to control and manage it as he sees fit. If he be not corrupt at the time of the entrusting, mightn't we have neglected the fact that he is human and temptation is no respecter of humans?

When the revolution is done and we re-erect our national storehouse, we will entrust it to a system of accountability in order to prevent theft and abuse.

The enemies of the revolution would emerge only when the revolution has started.

The enemies of the revolution would be those who would resist the wind of change because only a crook would want a chaotic and inefficient system to stand because it guarantees continuity of his criminal enterprise.

The enemies of the revolution would band together to resist the revolution and fight change because their best chance of continuing to perpetrate the rot is if the system is left untouched.

The enemies of the revolution will rise and declare that the country is fine the way it is and that it should be left alone.

They will call the revolution by many derisive names and do everything possible to make the revolution look like a force of evil rather than a force of good.

Against all odds, the revolution must be relentless and must persevere. The ordinary people who are the engine of the revolution have to know that they may never get another opportunity to change their country for good.

The revolution will not be a one-day or one-week or one-month event. It must be capable of sustaining for as long as it would take to secure victory.

The revolution must be well-funded if it is going to outlast the patience of those who will thumb their noses against it and hope that the ordinary people will sooner than later be wearied and dispirited by hunger and hopelessness.

The revolution must be persistent in the face of adversity and be willing to sacrifice blood in order to outlast the brutal force that would be unleashed against it.

The revolution has to be mobilized at the grassroots with proper messaging to ordinary people in their local communities who must be made to understand that the folks who purport to represent them politically are not serving their interests.

The people have to be made to understand that the wealth with which their representative is erecting a mansion right under their nose is loot from the national treasury which should have been for the people's use.

The people have to be made to understand that the big car and the lavish parties that the politician who is supposed to be serving them is enjoying is actually their share of the national cake that the politician has appropriated for himself.

The people have to be encouraged to lay claim to any bounty the politician has stored away for his personal use.

The big house and all the food in the house belongs to the people and the people are entitled to it.

The people must make the politician sufficiently aware that his days of free wheeling and self dealing are over and that he can no longer enjoy his loot in the comfort of his hometown and that henceforth whatever he brings home belongs to all.

The revolution must begin as a loud and peaceful effort to put the political elite on notice that the people are willing to forgive and forget past misdeeds but that going forward, the people will hold them accountable.

The tone of the revolution must be peaceful and the chant will be the same everywhere. The constant theme of the revolt must be "reforms now" "reforms now" "reforms now".

The revolution must be started by ordinary people forming and organizing revolutionary movements in their local communities, each with its local dynamics and each mounting protests in their local enclaves.

There would be protests in every corner of every town and at the doorstep of every government office and edifice.

The protests would be loudest in front of governors' mansions and legislative houses in every state, and uproarious at the national assembly and presidential palace in Abuja. Everywhere that the voice of the people can have effect, the revolution will pitch its tent.

The revolution should be all-inclusive. Labor unions, student organizations, market women, public employees, civil rights groups, trade groups and professional associations should be part of the revolution.

Grassroots revolutionary movements from one end of town will form alliances and coalitions with neighboring revolutionary movements and gradually build into regional and then national revolution.

As the revolution gathers momentum in local communities across the country and more and more revolutionary movements coalesce, it will be time for a showdown at the national arena.

By the time the revolution reaches Nigeria's capital, the politicians would already have been on notice and will either get out of the way or give in to the demands of the people.

There will be a temptation on the part of many to label an ordinary people's revolution in Nigeria as the actions of disgruntled elements of the society who want to create civil unrest in order to pursue personal agendas.

The revolution must be careful not to take on a negative tact in mounting its protests which will invariably alienate well-meaning Nigerians whose financial and logistic support it would need to succeed.

A people's revolution in Nigeria is potentially the only way to reform Nigeria because there is no indication that the political leadership in Nigeria is willing to act.

Reforms in Nigeria cannot be achieved by violence as exemplified by the actions of organizations like MEND. When a movement resorts to violence it undermines and undercuts the credibility of its cause.

No amount of car bombs and kidnappings and murders and assassinations and sabotages will be enough to dissuade and dislodge those who are committed to maintaining the corrupt status quo. As soon as one corrupt politician goes down there will be a thousand more of his ilk ready to take his place.

There is no edifice of repression and oppression that a peaceful, persistent and vibrant civil disobedience and agitation cannot bring down.

Violence only taints a noble cause. A good cause becomes bad if the means of achieving it becomes destructive.

Finally, it behooves every single Nigerian who has personal resources and who believes in the viability of Nigeria and the possibility of its redemption to join in the grassroots effort by contributing financially and morally to the revolution.

The benefits to be derived by transforming Nigeria from a corrupt, inefficient democracy that works for a few privileged people to an equitable, effectual democracy that works for all Nigerians will be well worth all the sacrifice and resources invested in a people's revolution.

PART IV

LETTERS TO FELLOW NIGERIANS

CHAPTER FIFTEEN

DEAR MR. PRESIDENT OF NIGERIA

HERE YOU ARE, SIR, IN a unique moment of history and of your life. You are in the most exclusive club in the world because very few people out of the nearly seven billion people in the world would ever have an opportunity to be the leader of anything much less a country as blessed and dynamic as Nigeria. For that I congratulate you from the bottom of my heart.

It is my humble guess that you fully appreciate the delicate position you have successfully landed yourself in and that you are fully capable and willing to render remarkable service on behalf of not just those who helped you get here but every single Nigerian for whom you are now a beacon of hope.

I am sure you have heard the wisecrack, "*uneasy lie the head that wears the crown*" and I'm sure you understand that your days on the high throne will indeed be uneasy. For that I sympathize with you.

Indeed, you occupy a very delicate position and the task in front of you is so daunting and onerous that you will need more than courage to carry you through. However, how you will be judged at the end of your days in office is entirely up to you.

You have two choices; one is to inscribe your name in gold and leave an indelible positive imprint on the checkered history of this great nation; the other is to blacken your name in soot and be relegated by history to the inglorious list of those who were called to serve but chose the path of ignominy and infamy.

Providence has hefted upon your shoulders a unique opportunity to build an eternal legacy and it would be foolish of you not to seize the moment to inscribe your name in gold.

It behooves me dear Sir, in case you have not been paying mind, to call your attention to the sad and ugly state of affairs in our dear country in the hope that you will be able to break the shackles of leadership and rise to the challenge of being the peoples' champion and redeeming the country from further deterioration.

My guess is, being that you have been privileged to traipse the hallowed corridors of power for a while now, that you are aware of the plunder and depredation and despoliation that our dear country has been subjected to for many many years.

I'm almost certain that like me, you have been sickened and overwhelmed by the wheeling and self-dealing and rancorous hoity-toity of political sorts all around you and you have wondered whether there is a future for our dear country.

Please do not kid yourself into thinking that because your government is not officially a dictatorship and because you have not been in power for thirty years or more the people have no cause to revolt against your government.

Quite on the contrary, the ordinary people of Nigeria have been subjected to dehumanizing and dispiriting economic repression and huge disparities in living standards that have made them question the very basis of their existence and rendered the status quo unsustainable.

I guarantee you, they have more than enough reasons to revolt and they would be more than justified to do so unless you do something about it.

I know, you are but one man and your hands may be somewhat tied because there were people who made your attaining the position you now occupy possible.

I know that you have made promises and you are beholden to certain powerful interests and party machinery which you cannot afford to cross and undercut.

I know you will be compelled to look the other way so that the leeches and vampires who expect rewards for throwing their muscle behind you can suck their fill from the already emaciated blood veins of your people.

I can imagine how tough it will be to resist and I am prepared to deal with the disappointment with a knowing shrug of the shoulder.

Sir, you have two paths in front of you and you will have to choose which one to follow. One will reward you with a pat on the back by an elite crop of old and new friends and the other will fetch you the adoration of the entire citizenry.

One path is a gold-adorned boulevard that will lead you to a serenade of fat-cat party hogs, robust-faced big-money backers, grateful friends and family, and greedy charlatans and other hangers-on. They all will, at the end of the day, be beaming and heaving with wide-lipped grins, thundering guffaws and hollow chuckles of satisfaction that you have delivered to them exactly what they wanted.

The other is a narrow thorn-ridden alleyway that will lead

you to the pained expressions of hopelessness and endless pangs of hunger and deprivation of ordinary folks who have suffered for years. At the end of the day, depending on what you do for them, they will either curse your name or bless it. And to them you will either be one more despicable vermin worthy of scorn or a messianic hero worthy of exaltation.

It is entirely up to you the path you choose but if my imploration is any useful, I would urge you to take the path that leads to heroism.

You need not look too far for the things you need to do to address the yearnings of the people. I urge you to reappraise the rot and vile all around and to urgently begin the arduous tasks of cleaning up the mess.

Perhaps you should start by picking up the Constitution upon which you have made an oath and try to make sense out of it.

I am convinced that when you have read through it, you will better appreciate the enormity of our country's woes and the full extent and range of what you need to do to change our country for the better.

I wish you well in the difficult journey ahead and pray that you succeed if you choose the right path.

I assure you that I shall be there in the end to see the outcomes of your deeds and I will, along with the rest of the ordinary folks, loudly proclaim and celebrate your heroism or bitterly curse the day you were born.

CHAPTER SIXTEEN

DEAR NIGERIAN POLITICIAN

CONGRATULATIONS TO YOU FOR SECURING the political office you now occupy after a hard-fought, contentious, all-or-nothing, no-holds-barred, do-or-die electioneering campaign. I am sure that in your mind, it is well worth it. If so, I'm happy for you.

Now that you are here, I know you are squared up for a showdown of a different kind at the end of which you hope to reap a thousand-fold what you have invested in cash and bags of rice and salt and sugar and vegetable oil to get here.

I am curious to know the sizes and number of suitcases you have brought along with you to your new office. I look at you and I can almost see the dollar and naira signs swimming around in your dreamy inner-thoughts and I imagine you are already snooping around looking for the keys to the treasury and wondering when the looting will start.

I see the glitter in your face and the glee in your eyes and I am wondering if there will be anything left when you are done.

I gave up hope and lowered my expectations when I saw the

things you had to do to get to where you are and concluded that you are no more different than many who had been before you.

However, I do want to appeal to the possibility that you still have a scintilla of conscience left and to remind you that the political office you now occupy is neither an entitlement nor your birthright. That the fact that you have been "elected" does not mean that you now own a country or a state or a local government and that everything in it now belongs to you.

In case you have forgotten, your political office demands much more than you think or expect and my intention here is to let you in on a few facts about the responsibility which you now shoulder.

Your job as an "elected" representative of the people is to serve and protect the interests of the people and nothing more.

The people's reasonable expectation from you are accountability, good governance and the basic necessities of life which include good roads, electricity, clean water supply and a fair playing field that ensures that they would be rewarded for their hard work; nothing more, nothing less.

I also wish to admonish you even before you have committed the first foul of your office that, in the event that you will not work towards ensuring a system that works for all rather than a privileged few, there is a wind of change starting to blow in the country that will guarantee that the old play book by which you and your ilk and predecessors have played will soon be updated.

In case you did not get the memo, things have changed considerably with the ordinary folks since the last time you paid any significant mind to their affairs. They have been down and out for so long and now they are beginning to stir to action because they cannot stand the shenanigans anymore.

First things first, I'm sorry to dash your hopes, but the looting will soon be over. The treasury will no longer be a free-for-all, do-as-you-like place that you can come to at will and at your convenience to stuff your suitcases with treasures that belong to all.

The days of freewheeling and self dealing will soon come to an end because our dear country is ready to hit the reset button.

The ordinary people whom you have fooled all these years to look the other way with bags of rice and salt and cans of sugar and vegetable oil while you loaded up your private accounts with treasures from our national vaults have become wiser.

They have caught on with your con-game and have realized that the interest you serve is not theirs. Now they are prepared to retake their country and you my friend are in for a rough ride.

Unless you pitch your tent with the people, you will soon realize that you are indeed in the wrong endeavor. You have squandered you personal resources and rigged your way to victory for nothing.

There will be no longer a place for political sorts whose primary ambition is to steal from our coffers. The days when politicians and public office holders steal the people blind and then turn around and flaunt their ill-gotten wealth are over.

And to ensure that it never happens again, we will institute real laws with real teeth and strict mechanisms for enforcing them.

Although we will not go the Draconian ways of China where the smallest bribe results in a date with the hangman, I can assure you that you will spend many years in prison for as much as thinking about embezzling public funds in Nigeria after all said and done.

I did not mean to scare you, Sir, but I hope my point is clear enough. However, I welcome you with open arms to work towards installing the kind of Nigeria that works for every Nigerian.

I know that even you are amenable to change and I am confident that you will embrace the peoples' revolution when it arrives at your doorstep.

However, in the event that you find it in your callous heart to resist, I beseech you to pack your suitcases and leave town for the wind of change that is starting to stir will neither know friend nor foe when it picks up momentum and sweeps into town.

The choice is yours.

CHAPTER SEVENTEEN

DEAR EX NIGERIAN GENERAL THINGAMABOB

YOU HAD YOUR DAY UNTIL not long ago when most of our young were still suckling in the bosoms of their mothers.

With iron fists and steel hearts you held us captive in the magic spell of your whim and took from us what was left of our collective dignities.

With highhandedness and absolute fiats you held sway without challenge and did as you saw fit things that till this day haunt us.

We heralded your comings with fear and trepidation and serenaded your departures with hopefulness and enthusiasm.

Again and again you came and went and again and again we persevered and prayed that your next coming would be your last and your last going would be your last.

Alas our prayers were heard and answered and by dawn's yawn we were brimming with long yearned-for exhilaration and hope that our new day will unfurl bright new promises.

We breathed a sigh of relief and welcomed new opportunities

with wide-armed warmth and caressed our new-found emancipation with cuddly love and hopeful euphoria.

You left the door ajar on your exeunt and although we noticed we did not mind considering that the circumstance of your departure assured that your return will not be soon.

In the madness of our euphoric bliss we imbibed your ought-to-be forgotten ways and neglected to make this day truly our own.

Even though we consider ourselves a different breed we embraced your filth, your wayward manners, and your crooked methods.

It is as though we are still shackled to your whims and that our so-called emancipation is only a figment of our imagination.

We glimpsed the black sheen of your boot in our closet and your starched, neatly-pressed uniform on the bed and somehow we were sure our minds were merely thick with hallucination.

Your footprints seemed fresh on the living room floor and a strong lingering scent of some alluring aftershave somehow made us feel like you are still nearby.

Maybe it is only a dream from which we will awake to discover that indeed you are gone.

Yet that shadow of yours on the wall seems very real and convincing.

Ah, but the door from whence you left remains ajar like it was never meant to shut you out.

Did you really leave or are you still hovering around the corner or lurking in the shadows?

Why is it that we still feel your cold and manipulative presence?

The room still smells like you and feels like you and still looks exactly the way you left it; boots in the closet, footprint on the floor, uniform on the bed, and all.

By the way, why did you leave your military gear behind?

Surely you could not have walked out without your brass tags and emblems and stars and naked.

Or did you?

Hey, wait a minute!

Who do we have here?

There you are!

You are still here!

In the room!

With us!

You never really left?

And now look at you!

That explains it all then; the pair of boots in the closet, the uniform on the bed, the accoutrements in the drawers, and footprints on the carpet!

You never left!

You merely swapped your uniform with civilian clothes so you can become like us and pretend to be us and roll with us.

What do you have there in your hands?

Puppet strings!

Loads of money for the piper!

The reins you never really gave up!

How clever of you to hoodwink us with your chicanery and make us believe that you would stay out of the frame of the portrait of our so-called new day.

We should have known when you handed us the keys and we inherited your props that the game would still be the same and that you would still be calling the shots.

However, today is realization's dawn as we finally pull the wool from over our eyes and set our compass for a course that is truly ours.

You are welcome to come along for the ride but the shots will henceforth be ours to call.

As we are swept up in the wind of change, your old props and the other things we inherited from you will be left behind in a cloud of dust.

Nota bene:

Sir, you had your chance and you blew it.

You had your opportunity but you did not use it wisely.

You had the unique privilege of inscribing your name in gold but you chose to blacken it in soot.

For many years you had the reins of power to use as you saw fit and your fit was to exploit and depredate rather than elevate and advance our country.

You did not have to consult anyone to make the rules all those years and the rules you chose to make only benefited you and your ilk.

You were like a tin-god who could by merely desiring it, have your way and the ways you had left our country decrepit and our people in tatters.

When you left, I was certain you were gone for good so that our country could rejuvenate in democratic flourish. But that would perhaps never be.

Why you still hang around befuddles me and why you still want to keep your fingers in the pie excoriates me.

I did not question all those years how it is that you were able to erect opulent mansions and massive estates that stretched from here to there with your soldier's salary.

What more do you want from a nation you despoiled without a care?

What more do you want to prove by meddling in and tampering with our fledgling democracy?

Why are you so obsessed to retake the reins of power?

Why can't you give our new day a chance to burgeon?

It is sad and truly disheartening that after all these years you are still very much in control and your members within our democratic trenches outnumber and outflank our civilian ranks by a margin of three to one.

Both here and there we have ex this and ex that now this and now that; wolves in sheep's clothing, all!

How can we truly institute change in our country when your ilk continues to maintain a stranglehold on the choices we make?

How can our country revivify when our democracy is actually your military regime in disguise?

If you did not do much for us when you wielded unquestionable and unchallengeable military powers how we can be sure that you will be able to do anything for us with less potent democratic powers?

Take a moment sir, to think hard for our country's sake about the choices you must now make.

Our people deserve true freedom and real change and a country that will work for all and not a privileged few as you and your ilk would prefer.

Change is coming to town whether you like it or not because it is time for the people to have their say.

We expect that you will roll out your might and your overflowing purse to resist but we are hopeful you will find a reason to desist.

We have forgiven the past and we are ready to embrace the future, a future that would work out just fine for both you and us.

If you must persist, persist but do not underestimate our will to insist until we have had our day.

If you must join our ranks, join, but the rules of the road will be the ones we write and not the ones you wrote in your heyday in military uniform.

CHAPTER EIGHTEEN

DEAR RANK AND FILE NIGERIAN POLICE AND NIGERIAN MILITARY

YOUR GUNS WILL BE POINTED in my face, your bullets will rip through my breast and my blood will be an effulgent carpet of red when the revolution comes to town.

They will order you to squelch and squash my fitful revolt and you will respond like an excited dog hearkening to a bone tossed in its front.

You will descend on revolution's square with your artillery and machine guns and you will be tempted to shoot first and ask questions later but my resolve will not be shaken.

They will instruct your top-guns from their cozy political edifices, your top-guns will summon you up from their palatial mansions and from your ramshackle overcrowded barracks you will spill into the street like rabid dogs to answer to their whim of crushing the will of the ordinary people who have come from homes not better off than yours to demand economic justice and fair polity.

Look amongst your ranks before you cork your rifle and shoot. In what way are you different from me? In what way am I the enemy?

You are an inconsequential rank-and-file gun-totting nobody who is exploited and economically repressed and controlled by your top-guns who have no regard for you.

I am an inconsequential ordinary citizen who is exploited and economically repressed and condemned to ugly fate by politicians who have no regard for me.

I urge you to take one good look at me before you set your cannons a-blast. Remember our common denominators; "exploited", "economically repressed", "inconsequential".

We share same sad story and same sad fate. You and me should be on the same side of the equation; my side.

Like me, you are struggling to make ends meet and like you I am a faceless, nameless nonentity who has to scrounge to survive while they ravish in opulence.

Like mine, your existence is rickety and basal and your life is nothing but a painful chapter on misery and abject poverty.

While they revel in exotic splendor and profligate bliss, we exist in substratal lowliness and make-do with mendicant endurance.

Like mine, your children have no future and like me you live from hand to mouth and dwell in hopeless hope that tomorrow will be better while their today is filled with excesses and their children have no worries about tomorrow.

Where are your wives? Do they still sit beside smoky kilns at the junction next to your barracks turning cobs of corn on red-hot charcoals or flipping bean cake balls in large frying pans filled with boiling oil in order to help make ends meet?

When was the last time your ends met? Or has beans become

so dear that your wives have been driven out of business and now there is no hope that the ends will ever meet?

Where are your children? Are they in school? Or have they been sent home because the school fees have not been paid? Did they eat any square meals yesterday or have they eaten any food today? Are they out hawking oranges or is it not the orange season yet?

What did you do with your last paycheck? Were you able to buy enough food for your family or did you use it to settle up last month's debt to the cut-throat vendor from whom you bought food and kerosene or firewood on credit?

Do you have running water or constant power supply? Do you buy food cheaper than the rest of us and do you travel on a different road than the decrepit roads the rest of us travel on?

What does the future hold for you?

Look at you, with your big guns and all. How much better than me are you?

How can you in all sincerity be willing to crush my spirit when we both are in the same shoes?

Why should you do the bidding of those who do not care for you and me and have taken for themselves the things which belong to you and me?

How can you justify your brutality towards me when we both belong in the same place; the dreg of society?

What will be your reward after you have snuffed me out and stifled the people's revolution?

Will they let you into their ranks and allow you a share of their obscene wealth?

Or will they let crumbs from their table of bounties flutter down to you in order to sustain your hunger and assure your blind loyalty?

Please, put down your guns and your batons and join the chorus of freedom and reform that rolls forth from revolution's midst.

The chance of a better future for you, your wife and children resides here amongst us your true ilk because salvation awaits us all at the end of our spirited struggle.

Do not put me down for their sake because it is not I who is destroying the country and the futures of its people.

Do not be a force and instrument of repression because you are also a victim of their high-handedness and waywardness.

In their eyes, you are worth nothing. You are mere attack dogs who would do anything to impress their master including eat their own.

In my eyes, you are worth more than you will ever know. You are one more sad reason why the revolution will come to town.

Chapter Nineteen

DEAR ORDINARY NIGERIAN

It is now up to you to challenge the status quo in Nigeria and bring an end to your woeful existence.

You can no longer afford to sit on the sidelines with your "*I don't care*" and "*e no concern me*" attitudes while your country is irreparably damaged by the wanton acts of those you call your leaders.

It is now your turn to have a say in how things should be in Nigeria.

Politicians have had their day. The crooks and highwaymen who have hijacked the reins of power have done their worst. The thieves and kidnappers and armed robbers who have turned your towns and villages and neighborhoods into free-for-all pillaging grounds have overstayed their welcome.

They all have relished enough in your complacence and indifference.

The days when public office holders lined their pockets with loot while you lived on prayers and despair are over.

The era of the shameless, in-your-face corrupt politician is at end.

The days of prosperity and economic liberation and good governance and security for all Nigerians are in the horizon.

And you my dear ordinary Nigerian will make that possible.

For far too long you have forgotten that you are the ones who really matter in this country.

For far too long you have taken for granted the fact that you are the ones whose labor and toil have milled the wealth upon which the wealthy political elite have feasted.

For far too long you have waited in vain for change to happen of its own accord.

For far too long you have wallowed in the improbable hope that the charlatans to whom you entrusted the affairs of your country will bring about the necessary change that will give your life new meaning and direction.

For far too long you have played the blame game and pointed accusing fingers without lifting them in protest.

For far too long you have decried and bemoaned the egregious vile and corruption and wanton abuse of office without rising in unison to do something about it.

This indeed is your moment.

It is the moment for action for every Nigerian who has dreamed of a homeland where he or she can feel safe and secure and be prosperous and free.

Your revolution will begin when you say so.

However, you cannot afford to wait.

You must act now with justifiable haste and frenetic fury.

Your revolutionary road will not be easy.

It will be weary and dispiriting and discouraging and daunting, but the rewards you will get if you stay the course will be well worth it.

Like everything good, there will be a price to pay.

It will not be a small price and it may even cost you your life but you must be ready, willing and able to pay whatever the price is.

They will try to dissuade you from the get-go and attempt to divide you with schisms of ethnicity and religious differences.

They will tell you the whole revolution is a ploy by a rival ethnic group and they will assure you that they are on your side.

You must not pay any mind to their divisive antics and you must treat their promises like the promises they made to you in the past which they never lived up to.

You must treat them with suspicion when they try to encourage you to fold your chairs and roll up your blankets and go home in the guise that they have heard your demands and will address them shortly.

Please, whatever you do, do not turn your revolution into an ethnic blame game.

Remember, we are all in this together.

We have suffered similar fates of deprivation and massive corruption at the hands of the same people, the political elite.

Have it at the back of your mind always that no matter where you have come from, whether from the east or the west or the south or the north, we have been denied opportunities and meaningful existence by the same people.

The ordinary Nigerian from Kaduna is not better off than the ordinary Nigerian from Enugu and the ordinary Nigerian from Abeokuta is not better off than the ordinary Nigerian from Calabar.

So do not let them fool you into thinking that your revolution is all about one ethnic group against another because it is not.

The theme of your revolution will be the same across the country because the suffering and the shabby condition of the existence of the ordinary Nigerian is the same across Nigeria; whether it is Kano or Warri or Ilorin or Umuahia. Whether you are Huasa or Igbo or Yoruba or Ijaw or Bini or Efik or whatever ethnic denomination you belong in, you have suffered the same economic repression.

Do not buy into their antics about your revolution being about one religion against another because it is not.

You are not worse off because you are a Moslem or Christian or whatever religious denomination you belong in. You have not enjoyed the benefits of a prosperous nation as you should because you are an ordinary Nigerian, period.

Your revolution must not be hijacked by crooks and criminals who will gravitate to your revolutionary grounds with intentions other than your own.

You must purge the trouble maker and the looter from your revolution the moment you spot them. Do not allow them to give your revolution a bad name.

You must be loud and vociferous and persistent and stubborn in your demands. Your voices will ring loud and clear from the center of your town so that shivers of fear will pierce deep in the hearts of those whose attention you seek to capture.

Your revolutionary song will be a song of change and you must carry your message of change with dignity and pride and be unyielding until the status quo gives.

You must be supportive to each other and share food and

drinks and comfort because you will be out in the revolutionary grounds for a while.

They will become irritated at some point especially when you have persisted and they will try to use force to disperse and destroy your revolution.

When the guns arrive, stand firm and tall and shoulder to shoulder and be unmoved and unnerved by the guttural barks of the men in black and their counterparts in green.

You must be stoic and un-intimidated and not give them an excuse to bludgeon or shoot you.

Your weapon of perseverance and peace will be ten times mightier that their machine guns and artilleries.

The flame of your revolution will not be put out until you have achieved your purpose. You will go home only when you demands have been met.

The day after your revolution, you will have good reason to celebrate.

A true government of the people for the people and by the people will be in place.

A government that is transparent and accountable to the people will be installed.

All the funds that would have disappeared into private accounts of corrupt politicians will be invested into infrastructure projects across the country that would pave the way for an explosion of industrial and manufacturing activities and your children's futures will be more secure.

An efficient rule of law mechanism will be in place and your rights and privileges will be assured.

Indeed, the revolution is for your own good. If you fail to seize the moment you will remain curst to a mediocre existence.

If you do nothing now, things will only get worse and not better and much like your present, your children's future will fade away in the murky mist of corruption and decay in the country you call your own.

Come all that hunger for change and a better Nigeria; let us get the revolution started. I wish you luck because you will need plenty of it.